COMING ALONG FINE

Coming Along Fine

Today's gay man and his world

Wes Muchmore and William Hanson

Boston · Alyson Publications, Inc.

This is a paperback original from Alyson Publications, Inc., PO Box 2783, Boston, MA 02208.
Distributed in England by GMP Publishers, PO Box 247, London, N15 6RW.

First U.S. edition, March 1986
ISBN 0 932870 92 9

Contents

Introduction

The simple act of coming out eliminates a lot of problems in a gay man's life. However, as he continues in his new existence, the gay man will find himself faced with challenges and situations that he once never dreamed existed.

In this book we deal with a number of these difficulties: a gay man may become bored with his mode of life, or he may encounter problems in relating with lovers, family, and friends; men who are not completely out have to deal with special stresses; for all of us the straight world is not always easy to get along with; and AIDS imposes additional long-term anxieties.

We also explore a number of facets of the newly evolving gay world in chapters on politics, business, travel, law, and entertainment. We consider, as well, how some of the venerable gay traditions are faring at present, and how both the old and the new can offer opportunities for a richer life.

Our previous book, *Coming Out Right: A Handbook for the Gay Male*, was written for the man new to gay life and having little knowledge of its ways. There we strove for neutrality, offering the clearest "road map" we could to help newcomers understand the basics. In this volume, however, we address the gay man who knows his world, who has a basic familiarity with gay existence, and so we feel free to express our opinions in areas of controversy and, in some instances, to indulge our sense of humor.

Our hope is that, rather than necessarily coming to share our points of view, you as the reader will develop your own useful insights into matters of importance to you in living your gay life.

Wes Muchmore
William Hanson

I
Plights and Pressures

PLIGHTS AND PRESSURES

1 Bored, Bored, Bored

> Of the pleasures and goods we have, there is none exempted from some mixture of evil and incommodity.
>
> — Montaigne

Let's start with the problem which may be the most prevalent among experienced gay men – becoming bored with the gay world, finding this existence limited and not very satisfying.

Boredom can appear in many guises: a lack of a sense of purpose, a feeling that one is contributing nothing useful to the world, a sense of living a meaningless life that is repetitious and dull.

For one of our friends the realization struck all at once, on the dance floor. Nothing had changed from the other weekend nights he'd been there. He was seeing the same sexy guys and hearing the same music. But in an instant he didn't care about it any longer.

Sometimes the process is more gradual. Another friend of ours, a few years older, began to dread making his customary stop at his favorite bar. His acquaintances there, once so bright and witty, had nothing to say he hadn't heard many times before. Worse, he saw that many of them were simply drinking their lives away in a pointless ambience of mild bonhomie, gossip, and cruising.

Gay drift

Many gay men feel that the bar-baths-party route is all there is and that even if they're bored out of their minds with it, there's no other choice but loneliness and celibacy. Some do realize that there are alternatives in the gay world but hold back from exploring new possibilities for themselves. This is true of older men especially, those who were trained in the codes and cautions of the Bad Old Days. They may find it difficult to step forth into the new gay world, all so open and brightly lit.

A goodly number of men feel that even if the life that was so attractive at twenty-five seems unsatisfying a few years later, it is still the life they want to lead. For them, anything else would mean change, which would mean that time is passing, which would mean that they are – horrors! – growing *older*.

Some of us react to our boredom with a feeling that we have failed in our lifestyle, that we are not sufficiently into it or up to it. So we try harder, hoping that once we complete our crash diet and regain our ability to get into 28" jeans, all the satisfactions of yesteryear will come flooding back. That is, we continue living as we have lived not because it makes us feel good but because we want to avoid feeling bad.

Probably stronger than ignorance and fear, and certainly reinforcing them, is habit. As a friend put it, "I just *had* to go to the bar every night or so. If I didn't go I got the feeling that I wouldn't know what was going on, and that this was somehow sort of threatening. Of course there was nothing going on."

Oh Mary, the truth is...

Let's take a closer look at these reasons for just going along day by day while enjoying life less and less. First, the bar–bath–dance-hall life and the ghetto existence are not all there is to the gay world. These most prominent and easily available areas of gay life serve very narrow interests. Amusement, status, protection and company may be provided, but only incidentally: the real goals are partying and sex.

Dwellers in the gay ghettos are a minority of the total gay population and, by comparison, extremely transient. In some ways gay ghettos serve as finishing schools for newly out, usually younger, gay men. We have discovered in our travels that many a denizen of Podunk's only gay bar will have spent a few years living in some locale like the West Village or the Castro, later to return to what they consider a less frantic environment.

That is, the gay ghettos are full of men who are going through an adolescence they were not allowed to enjoy, or didn't dare to have, when they were fifteen. After years of suppressing desires and feeling alone and guilty, many men find gay ghetto life delightful and fulfilling. As a complete way of life for most or all one's years, though, it can only be considered very unbalanced.

The idea of the bar and the ghetto as the center of the gay universe – what we might call the castrocentric point of view – is reinforced strongly by the media. The majority of gays living outside gay neighborhoods are invisible to reporters from mainstream press and television. And many gay writers themselves, in both fiction and factual material, present us with a vew of gay life that is all-ghetto.

In addition, gay businesses, if their ubiquitious advertising were to be believed, would convince us that the commercial gay culture *is* the gay world.

The twit. Those who do not agree that the bar-bath scene and ghetto life answer to only a few of most gay men's needs should consider the perfect product of these particular areas of gay life, the man who is completely satisfied by it all.

We give you the Twit.

This is a type that has always been with us. Regrettably but inevitably, some of us are born Twits and can't manage anything more. No brain, no pain, as the saying goes. Lately, however, taking full advantage of the gains of gay liberation, the Twit's numbers have radically increased.

We believe recruits come from two sources. First, a Twit's existence does have a certain appeal; it's a way of life that makes do without real feelings, real problems, and, well, real life. Many a gay man drifts into a state of Twitdom unknowingly. He starts out playing the role of Twit, in order to go with the flow in the bars and the boogies. And he finds it's kind of easy and relaxing to be just a cute sex object with only fun in mind.

Second, since Twits are everywhere, no doubt many a

newly out gay man is led to conclude that Gay Twit equals Gay Man, then patterns his behavior accordingly.

Nobody is perfect, and we all have our twitty moments, but the stone Twit, though he comes in all shapes, sizes, and ages, is easily identified:

1. As far as the senses go, the Twit has definite peculiarities. First, verbally he limits his vocabulary almost wholly to one word. That word is *really*. This saves the effort of displaying any feelings about the subject under discussion or of even pretending to listen to what someone else is saying. And *really* is a word that can easily be shouted over highly amplified music.

Aurally, Twits have hearing problems. They become aware of what another says only when certain subjects are dealt with:

a. oneself (body, clothes, hair; compliments only);
b. scandal about somebody famous, preferably in show business;
c. sex, in general;
d. getting it on, specifically.

Visually speaking, the Twit cruises incessantly and everywhere, not excluding his mother's funeral.

And tactilely, the Twit gropes a lot.

2. Socially the Twit's uncompromising motto is "packaging über alles." When another man meets his criteria in the physique, youth, and looks departments, the Twit can be very nice. But if, perhaps at some social gathering, an older gay man is being civil, the Twit will interpret mere manners as a heavy come-on and respond with sudden rudeness. This he dignifies with the word *attitude.*

3. In the love department the Twit fucks expertly. Emotionally, however, he's underfunded. His lovemaking will not be *molto expresivo*, however good, and a long-term affair is out of the question. He would find himself overdrawn in less than a week. Besides, he lacks the necessary concentration. That's why he changes his unlisted phone number every couple of months, to clear the half-remembered tricks out of his life.

4. Mentally, the Twit has either or both of two kinds of intelligence: low or unused.

*

Old dogs, new tricks. An unwitting descent into twittery is not the only pitfall for gay men. Those who came of age when the gay world was a mostly secret and sometimes dangerous place often have fears and responses that are based on past experience and not, in many cases, on present conditions. In order to enjoy the wider opportunities in the New Gay World, many men will only have to readjust their mind-sets a little. Others may have to make a strong conscious effort. A friend of ours who came out in the Bad Old Days went to the trouble of making a list of activities, starting with those he considered least threatening and ending with those he worried about the most. Then, over a period of a year or so, he tried them all, roughly in order. One of his more daring efforts was to join in a gay political march. Afterwards he told us, "I never dreamed I'd walk down the main drag of this city with a gay-rights picket sign in my hands. On the one hand, I kept expecting to get killed, and on the other, I felt wonderful."

Not getting any younger, dearie. It's true that we live in a youth culture, something Asians and Europeans find rather odd about Americans, and certainly having looks in good condition and being non-old count for a lot in the gay world. Gays have found a variety of ways to not face the facts of aging.

Let's begin with the man who refuses to age gracefully, choosing to fight it every inch of the way. We don't refer to the person who merely takes good care of himself; we speak of the gay landmark preservationist. At forty-five or fifty this man looks almost exactly as he did back in his twenties – assuming you don't look too closely – with clothing, hair style, and manner, all so winning when he came out, remaining very much the same.

This masquerade often enough turns into the great nightmare figure of gay men – the old queen. The once attractive face is haggard, decked with rococo eye bags and perhaps touched up with 'invisible' makeup, and what hair remains is always some bright, unlikely shade, combed desperately over the huge bald spot. The man's temperament is uneven, ranging from chatty to bitchy to snarling to tearful.

This living sacrifice to the pressures and limitations of being gay is a far less common sight than in past years, but in many variations is still with us.

Copping out. Some men, feeling they no longer rate in the gay world, opt out of it. This is visible in what has been called the male menopause, which can set in even as early as, say, age thirty. "It's too late for me," goes the reasoning. "Why should I bother with diet and exercise, with watching my drinking, with keeping up social obligations?" Slowly becoming a slob, this man takes stock of himself every so often, sees more and more reason to be unhappy, and lets neglect reign.

Some men, whether they suffer male menopause or not, bit by bit become loners. They read more and more, see a lot of movies and television, and often vastly ritualize their existences. Everything goes in a certain place, everything is done at a certain time in a certain way. Busyness not only fills in the loner's hours, but his life patterns effectively exclude other people – who'll only upset his routines – and so they reinforce his solitude.

Then there are those older gay men who take the radical step by playing it straight. Typically they are not all that much out of the closet, prefer to live the double life once common among gays, work in the white-collar world, and socialize a good deal with heteros.

Checking out. Of course there is just plain self-destructing. Whatever way a man chooses, as an old queen, a slob, a loner, or a "straight," he may come to depend excessively on booze or drugs – "Goin' down slow," as the old blues song puts it.

The ultimate step is suicide. The classical stereotype is of a man once gorgeous but no longer, feeling that without the party, life is nothing, and that for him the party is over. In the time-honored pattern he checks into a sleazy hotel and washes a mass of pills down his throat with a large amount of alcohol.

Many gay men do handle aging well, but for those who don't, the important thing is to realize that it's not a matter of joining a monastery or getting a series of facelifts or writing a note that begins, "Farewell, cruel world."

It's more a matter of accepting a few truths. First, everybody is getting older. Nobody is alone in aging. Second, life is not just youth. Many a young man doesn't understand that ten, twenty, or thirty years onward he may have interests that are almost completely different from those of his younger days. Third, pure physical attraction is not usually the basis for enduring relationships. Something that lasts can't be based on something that doesn't. The younger gay man, especially, is wise to school himself to look for attractive qualities in others aside from the obvious physical ones. Hots may rule for a good while, but other characteristics can have their influence as well, if a man lets them, like charm, kindness, intelligence, and sensitivity.

Laying blame. If a man blames himself for being bored with his style of life, this means essentially that he is accepting his small area of the gay world as the whole thing. He's judging his own needs against the limitations of his environment, which is most definitely getting the cart before the horse.

Habits are tenacious, but they can be broken. There's no easier way to do this than to find new interests. It's hard to slip back into old routines if you are busy with finding ways to enjoy your life.

Doing something

As the playwright Harvey Fierstein said, "Gay liberation should not be a license to be a perpetual adolescent. If you deny yourself commitment, then what can you do with your life?"

Exactly. And the first commitment a man should have is to himself. The old idea that a gay life has to be a tragic or frivolous one doesn't hold any more. Most of the built-in excuses of the Bad Old Days have faded away.

In general a man should cultivate as much detachment about his life as he can, facing facts and taking a realistic viewpoint. In avoiding self-delusion, however, a man has to be careful not to go too far in the other direction, turning his problems into weapons for a self-hating attack on himself.

A man should not only decide what changes he wants to make but also in what order. Adjusting everything all at once means sure defeat. Then – and this is the hard part – he should begin to make the changes. Here he will probably have to battle the great human tendency to put things off.

Rearrangements may well excite a certain amount of stress, irritability, anxiety, or insecurity. The best way to deal with this is to set one's mind ahead of time to the expectation of having to grin and bear it for a brief period, until the changes begin to be rewarding and old habits are modified or broken.

Merely sticking a toe in the water and calling it a good try is not making a real effort. If, for instance, you join an interest group and find out it's run by a small clique who expect everyone else to produce effort and money but keep their mouths shut, you may quit, disillusioned . . . but you shouldn't then damn *every* interest group as being the same.

The effort to realign your life may be strenuous, but there is an extra reward for going to the trouble: the achievement will give you a lot of good feelings about yourself, and this will make future changes all the easier.

PLIGHTS AND PRESSURES

2 Gay Husbands

> Love demands certain things as a right. . . .
>
> — Henry James

The long-term lover relationship between gay men can be exquisitely rewarding in terms of affection, companionship, and supportiveness, but it is also notoriously difficult to maintain.

Partly this is because there are so few external pressures to stay together. Rarely do two men *have* to continue as a couple for the sake of the children, for religious, social, or dynastic reasons, or because one partner hasn't the skills to make a living outside the home.

And partly, it's the result of a lack of roles and rules to follow within a gay relationship. The lovers have to work it out for themselves.

In addition, gay men often face two further problems that are peculiar to their life situation. First, many a man expects too much from his lover — all the affection he perhaps didn't receive earlier in life, the attention and support he may have been denied because he was "different" in childhood.

Second, even gay men go for the macho trip, play strong and silent and hide their emotions. They don't want to appear weak in front of anyone, especially not another man. But in a gay lover relationship this front can be kept up only at the sacrifice of intimacy and communication. Human involvements cannot flourish unless they are carried on in a manner consistent with what we know about human nature. A few verities may help lovers maintain a successful long-term pairing:

1. *Love rarely starts out even.* At the beginning of a relationship the partners are not likely to be equally in love. This may seem obvious, but many a man who is madly enamoured blithely assumes his partner is in the same exalted state. Finding out differently often breeds disillusion. But people don't always know their own feelings clearly, and many pairings that begin unequally do fire up very well. The trick is to have faith but not blind faith, whether you are the partner who is sick with love or the partner who is not yet sure if this is "it" or not.

After a while a distinct danger arises: if one of the couple merely goes along with the relationship without developing a distinct interest in it, the prognosis is for a slow and often painful death.

2. *Lovers rarely perceive their relationship as fifty-fifty.* The awful truth is that we human beings accept any number of things done for us without thinking we have received a favor. This may stem from a deep, basic need to confirm to ourselves our importance as individuals, but in a lover relationship this means that each partner, even though contributing equally, may easily be convinced that he is doing more than his share.

Obviously this is a quirk of human nature that can breed resentments, misunderstandings, even hostilities. As a rule of thumb, if you see the relationship as 55-45 or even 60-40, chances are it's really pretty much 50-50. If you feel it's 90-10, that spells trouble ahead. When even *you* can see that your partner is putting a good deal more into the relationship than you are, well, shape up quick, or enjoy it while you can.

3. *One-sided relationships don't survive.* Obvious as this sounds, the situation can evolve without either party initially being aware of it. He who loves the more may all too willingly assume responsibilities at the beginning of a relationship which become burdensome and excessive later on, when passion has leveled off to simple loving and caring.

It's essential to recognize that "burdensome responsibilities" can encompass just about anything, from being saddled with the laundry and housework to merely always having to be the one who decides what the couple will do when they go out. In human relationships trivial items can be exceedingly important. It's not disagreements about U.S. foreign policy that cause resentment to build up, it's spats about taking out the garbage.

4. Relationships require a shared outlook in order to last. We all know of successful long-term pairings in which the partners appear to have little in common, where the only obvious explanation is that opposites attract.

Certainly they do, to a degree. As Donald Vining has observed, "an opera-lover encountering someone who can't abide the art form may be bowled over that the person . . . can build shelves and cabinets with an ease that is quite beyond him." Blue collar–white collar relationships and interracial ones may well thrive on the attractiveness of differences.

However, in any ongoing gay relationship there is inevitably a substantial identity in the partners' objectives and in their attitudes to daily living. Sometimes the shared outlook that cements the relationship may escape general notice. Perhaps a couple's mutual life objective may consist of nothing more cosmic than an obsession with decorating their shared home. Often enough the outside observer can see only the differences, but close inspection of long-term pairings almost always reveals a similarity in approaching life and shared or at least highly compatible objectives.

Rx for ailing relationships

A basically good relationship can begin to unravel for any number of reasons, and it's wisest to try to do something about it as soon as possible.

Successful gay couples communicate well. If there are problems, the best thing is to sit down together and talk them out. This doesn't mean argue, tempting as that may be. It means that hair should be let down, that frankness and clarity should be the goal. Some men hesitate to do this for fear of making matters worse. But what else can make them better?

If a couple has gotten along well enough in the past but feel the relationship has gone flat, it may be that their interests have diverged in such areas as social life, entertainment, hobbies and other ways they can spend their time. Generally, if the two men basically respect each other and each is willing to compromise, this shouldn't be too great a problem.

Gay couples who find they argue constantly over small matters should try to figure out together what they are *really* upset about. Trivial bickering may be a matter of personality differences, but often it masks some deeper problem in the relationship, one which the partners have been unwilling to confront.

Frequently the subject lovers need to discuss is sex, and many men find this hard to do. But bed problems, like any others, will not go away just because they're being ignored. Often lovers don't want to face the almost inevitable lessening of sex interest between them. But it seems to us that it's better to discuss new approaches, new areas that could be investigated, than say nothing and let the relationship founder. Some gay men never get beyond this difficulty, so they don't realize what exquisite pleasures can be devised with someone whose body and sensual responses are familiar.

Talking out problems may be rather painful, but it can help, and may bring surprising enlightenments: "I never realized you cared about *that,*" or "*My* friend? I always invited him because I thought *you* liked him," or "You mean you *prefer* me with this additional weight on?"

It's true that a frank discussion can be a big factor in bringing a relationship to an end. But isn't that better than letting it drag on and on, getting uglier and less satisfactory as it goes?

Cyclics and steady-staters. Every couple is different. Some hassle each other a lot, yet have a basically strong relationship. Others hardly ever raise their voices at each other. The variations are immense in number. However, there do seem to be two basic approaches to lover relationships. One we can call the steady-state pattern. The pair constantly adjusts and corrects for difficulties and misunderstandings, making an effort to keep the relationship moving smoothly along.

The other is the cyclical approach. That is, the lovers just adore each other for a time, then enter a dish-throwing phase, ending with a grand reconciliation and a return to the adoring-each-other state.

The steady-stater may feel that a cyclical lover is bent upon wilfully tearing apart a carefully constructed relationship. The two types can get on, though, if each knows where the other is coming from. If the cyclic can understand that love is not always expressed at the top of one's voice, and if the steady-stater can see the noisy moments as part of a Greater Whole, then with a little mutual understanding and the occasional purchase of a cheap set of dishes, there should be no real problem.

Breaking up

Of course there are lovers who should break up. We think a rule to follow is that there's no chance for lovers if they can't make it as mere roommates.

Sometimes a relationship actually turns destructive, with abusiveness, perhaps heavy drinking or doping, maybe physical mayhem. Needless to say, any couple moving toward this sort of interaction should immediately split and remain far apart. The danger here is that lovers can be bound tightly to each other by negative aspects of their personalities. Such couples typically tend to live in social isolation and concentrate on destroying themselves. Apart, they are likely to function well. Together, usually for obscure psychological reasons, they are poison.

While it's true that these relationships often are strong and do indeed fulfill some basic needs, it's also true that intensity isn't everything.

Hard to do. There is no easy way to break up, but some approaches are less gruesome than others. The first thing to recognize, though unfortunately many splitting couples don't see it at all, is that if it's really the end of the line, there is nothing more to argue about. Oh, the desire may be there, but why bother, since now it serves no good end?

It's best to avoid the cast-of-thousands finale. If a break-up means battle scenes every time paths cross, if friends are forced to take sides, then the couple hasn't really let the relationship run its course. They should be encouraged to get back together, or duel to the death at dawn, or figure out some other way of at least showing consideration for their friends and neighbors.

One good way to end the affair is to do it in two separate

steps. That is, separate the it's-over speech from the act of moving out. This will minimize, for both of you, such lines as "That's *my* record, not yours!" or "I didn't give that to you, I just let you wear it," or "Well, I don't want to get rid of that broken-down old couch either."

When the time comes to sort out possessions, both parties should bend over backwards to be fair. "*Your* record? Oh. Well, here." Proceeding thus, the steam is taken out of one's feelings toward the former amour, so one doesn't feel so bad. The ex is less threatened, has less reason to become angry and more motivation to cooperate. Proceedings may even develop a slight competitively cooperative edge: "Why don't *you* keep the record; you like it better than I do."

Advantage can be taken, of course, but a polite approach is much wiser than conducting the leave-taking as though it were the shootout at OK Corral. Behaving well in this situation is not only classy, it's time-saving, good for the memories when one looks back, and it may save grief and lawyer's fees in larger matters, such as the home, the antiques, the business.

Life, as most everyone has noticed, is not an MGM musical, and nobody is guaranteed to live happily ever after. On top of all that, a good man is hard to find. So when two good men do find each otheer, they should expect to have to put some work into their relationship if they want it to become a feature-length, all-star, award-winning production.

PLIGHTS AND PRESSURES

3 Relativity

> Understanding is not loving; being loved does not entail being understood.
>
> — Seymour Kleinberg

Five gay men, friends ages 35 to 52, were having dinner together. One of them mentioned that he'd recently gone back to see his family for the annual visit. "Before I went," he said, "I called and talked with Mother, telling her I couldn't eat high-cholesterol foods any more and that I'd appreciate her keeping this in mind – the first dinner's always a huge one."

Our friend – we'll call him Bill – arrived at his parents' to find that dinner consisted entirely of dishes made with lots of eggs, fat, cream, butter, and beef.

"I thought we'd settled all the ugly stuff years ago," he said, "but there it was, the dark side of it, spread all over the dining room table. Mother killing me softly and not even aware of it."

Bill's lover Raymond has a mother who adores him. She is a widow who raised him in loving but stern righteousness in the small-town south. After Raymond moved to California, his mother came to visit fairly frequently, and often insisted on rearranging some aspects of his life for him. Because of his own need for space and freedom, and because of Bill, Raymond bought her a small apartment building in her home town. Managing it keeps her busy, providing an outlet for her leadership abilities.

Martin, like Bill, faithfully visits his parents every year. He thoroughly dislikes his mother, who has problems which as an adult he now understands. As a child, though, he found them extremely hard to live with, as when she blamed him, age six, for the ruin of her life. Martin goes through the brief annual charade for the sake of his father, whom he loves dearly. He's long since come to understand why the man worked overtime so much and saw so little of his son during his childhood.

Leo hasn't seen his parents since he was eighteen. His father was a cruel, brutal man, "probably psychotic," Leo says, and his mother was a spineless, masochistic worshipper of his father. "I ran out screaming," he says, "and I haven't been back since. It was tough at first. Being raised inside their madness was a lousy preparation for dealing with the world, but if I hadn't left I'd have committed suicide."

Charles, in his fifties, lives with his mother, a widow, as he has all his life. Until recently she took care of all the details of their existence, but age and illness have made her too frail to continue. Charles wouldn't dream of putting her in a convalescent home, and his nights out have become rare events. He has never told his mother anything about his sex life, and she blithely thinks of him as perfect, if sometimes a little inattentive.

Frank always got along well enough with his parents until his mother died. Since then his father has made efforts to know his youngest son better. As Frank says, "It's kind of late. He taught my older brothers how to swim, but he never got around to me. I had to learn at the Y. In junior high my mother had my father go with me to the athletic department's award banquet. I won some big prize, I can't remember for what, and he didn't say a word about it, nothing. A day or so later I learned that my father told my mother how proud he was of me. But he didn't tell *me*. . . . Nothing in itself, but it's the whole story of my father and me in a nutshell." Frank visits his father at regular intervals, as a duty. "That's more than my brothers do, so maybe that's why he wants us to be pals now."

Straights have problems in relating with their families, too, but it does seem that difficulties are greater for gays. Not only does the gay man have to decide whether to tell his parents about his sexual orientation, but, as we see it, some difficulties arise from the fact that the gay child all along relates differently to his mother and father than does the heterosexual child.

Mind drama. Until recently the prevailing theory of homosexuality held that an overwhelming mother and underwhelming father combined to cause a child to become interested in his own sex. This idea is now much in question. More and more evidence suggests that homosexual people are born that way, or possibly become so shortly after birth. If this is the case, then the problems gays so often experience in relating with their parents may have their beginnings in the great, unconscious Oedipal drama every child is thought to play out with his mother and father.

Classically, the male child is said to wish to possess his mother. When he comes to realize that his father cannot be vanquished and replaced by himself, the son decides to do the next best thing: imitate Pop's ways, become big and strong as he is, and finally marry "a girl just like the girl that married dear old Dad."

However, for the the male child who is gay, whether he or anybody else knows it, Dad might be as much or more interesting to possess than to copy, and Mom, since she does have Dad, may be more or less worth imitating.

The visible effect can be that of a boy who is somewhat effeminate, passive, and interested in "female" activities. Mom may find her son quite a pal. Father, unconsciously sensing the threat of both homosexuality and incest, may react by becoming rather distant with his son. As time goes on, if the boy shows clear signs of being a sissy, father's rejection may increase, reinforcing the child's closeness to his mother.

Thus it may appear that a boy is overmothered, being made into a sissy, while the reality is something quite different.

The validity of this scenario can't be guaranteed, but certainly it's frequent for gay men to have poor communication with their father and an exaggerated, if not always placid and healthy, closeness with their mothers.

No matter what

Children generally suppose parental love to be unconditional. Fiends on death row get visits from their mothers, who emerge in tears, telling the press their Igor is really a good boy and didn't mean to hurt all those blind schoolchildren he bludgeoned to death. Many a father, often for years and in tolerant or martyrish silence and at considerable expense, gets his erring sons out of scrapes with the neighbors, the schools, underage females, and the law.

The gay son who reveals his way of life to his parents, however, is testing severely the limits of their love, and often they fail the exam. Sometimes there is an extreme reaction that most non-gay people think exists not in reality but only in Victorian plays: "Out! And don't come back!"

Even parents who try to understand and accept may grow distant from their son, and this is particularly true of fathers. Relations may be strained, become extremely informal, even fade away to almost nothing.

Generally speaking, "telling them" is more customary, if not yet universal, among the younger generations of gay men. Older men, despairing of being understood and accepted, usually have chosen to say nothing. To be able to indulge in their lifestyle discreetly, they often live far away from their parents. Communication tends to be minimal, careful ("Hide those magazines!") and not very fulfilling except for the sense of duty.

Open about his way of life or not, many a gay man has his own resentments stemming from the family experience. It's not realistic to blame one's homosexuality on one's parents, but many men do this. Some feel that being gay forced them to get out on their own too early in life. Others believe a brother or sister was dearly loved while they were barely tolerated.

Mending the breach

All in all, among gay men there are a lot of weak or broken lines of communication with parents and other members of the family as well. Many prefer to leave things as they are. But others, where time has healed wounds and blurred ugly memories, often wish to re-establish contact "before it's too late."

A lot of thought should be given before any action is taken, we feel. Anyone who wants past injustices recognized, expects abject apologies for mistreatment and rejection, or seeks blanket approval for his way of life, is likely to be thoroughly disappointed. In this world a lot of emotional bills are due that never get paid, because everybody makes out accounts by his or her own reckoning.

If a man misses his parents, it's a rough rule of thumb that the more years without contact, the more he has idealized them. This presents obvious dangers: dear, delicate Mom may turn out to be a foul-mouthed old bat, and Dad, all tweedy and wise, could be spending his sunset years liquefying his pension check and running it through his long-suffering liver. On the other hand, the monsters of the tough old days of a gay man's youth may actually be quite lovely human beings.

The terms of the rupture with the family should be considered. If the parents felt their son "betrayed the family" by "going gay," then the likelihood is that they still feel this way. But if the break occurred in an outburst of anger, chances for re-establishing rapport may be fairly good: tempers do cool, regrets could be felt, understanding may have increased.

Chances are not so good if the break took a long time and was accompanied by all sorts of neurotic snarlings and undertones. And success should not be expected if either parent is gifted with definite mental problems. The failure rate is high as well if the mother's reaction to the son's gayness was stronger than the father's. Though this isn't common, it does happen, usually where Mom puts a high value on conformity, appearances, or social position.

Religious fundamentalists are hard to predict. If their faith is deep and not merely an excuse to indulge in bigotry, it may give them some means of accepting their son as he is. Either way, however, they are likely to show clearly their true feelings at the first contact. This can be a great help in deciding whether to go any further.

Taking the step. Assuming a man wants to try to re-establish contact, the approach he chooses should be given careful thought. The most direct – and worst – way is to bound up their steps, ring the bell, and when the door opens say, "Hi, folks! It's me, your long-lost son."

It's best to avoid surprises. A telephone call would be wiser, and a letter better yet. Sometimes a sympathetic relative or friend can act as a contact between the gay man and his parents.

For very iffy reunions, the Just Passing Through number is a good idea. Son arranges to meet parents between planes, in some neutral public territory, like the airport coffee shop, where the public setting would discourage the throwing of scenes. If things work out, further meetings can be planned. If not, the loss in time is small, and no new ugly scenes will have to be added to the mind's collection of old ones.

Timing and occasion should be carefully considered. Holidays, birthdays, anniversaries, or funerals may or may not be good times to re-establish contact. Sometimes communication becomes easier after a death or divorce. If Father's implacable ire caused the break, with Mother aghast and wringing her hanky, then as a widow she might be more than willing to see her boy again.

Whatever the arrangements, it's best to meet parents alone. It may be tempting to have the support of a lover or a friend, but his presence is going to minimize real communication and otherwise complicate matters.

It's wise to be prepared for a possible second rejection, or at the least the almost inevitable small understanding of gay life, and, of course, for just plain disappointment.

The eternal son

Sometimes gay men are not troubled by separateness from family, but by excessive closeness. Day by day interdependence grows, especially with mother, to the point that as an adult the son remains in the parental home. He takes over the duties, this side of scandal, of a husband, or perhaps simply continues as an aging son.

The gay man in this situation finds it difficult, probably impossible, to participate fully in gay life or develop a deep relationship with another gay man. Yet some are happy this way, protected from a way of life that, deep down, they fear.

Other gay men feel trapped. Sometimes unfortunate circumstances, usually illness, leave no room for choice, but we suspect that most often a man is trapped by his own feelings. It's probably better that he sort them out and that he recognize the difference between helping his parents and signing his life over to them. Commonly these men veer between strong resentment and the feeling that it's better they be unhappy than Mom or Dad. But a man like this is guilt-tripping himself into continuing an untenable arrangement, which means he is setting himself up for a lot of empty, bitter years ahead.

Such a dear

The Uncle Charlie syndrome is how we describe the other big problem that gay men can get into with their families. Charming, presentable, always a pleasure to have at the big family gatherings, Uncle Charlie is dependably good for a touch, listens patiently to tales of trouble and woe, steers junior to a summer job, and helps in a big way when the kids have fees to pay at Harvard or Juilliard.

Many Uncle Charlies are genuinely appreciated, respected, and loved by their families. Others know they are buying affection and not getting their money's worth in return. Even so, from obscure motivations and vague guilts they can't clearly explain, they feel obligated to continue in the role.

Some Uncle Charlies, aware they are being used, prefer to let well enough alone. For those who don't there are two cures, both fairly painful:

Uncle Charlie can announce that financial reverses have struck, that he faces ruin, and that he needs a small loan.

If family members rally to help bail out Charlie's sinking boat, he can congratulate himself on having a lovely bunch of relatives. If they don't. . . .

The second remedy requires no lying and takes very little time, but it can be far more gruesome: Charlie simply arranges to listen behind a door after he leaves a room full of relatives. When he's heard what they say about him behind his back, he can decide if he has been foolishly generous or not. Then he can tiptoe away, go to his lawyer's, and make some changes in his will. That should help him feel a little better.

Our first relationships in life may be the most influential, but that doesn't mean they're always the healthiest. Even with love and the best will in the world, parents and their gay children may have great difficulties in communicating with one another. While gay men have to accept that certain problems come with the territory and must be borne, they should not confuse these difficulties with others that can be lessened or alleviated. Nor should they allow themselves to think that their sexual orientation requires an extraordinary sacrifice of their lives in favor of others.

PLIGHTS AND PRESSURES

4 Ours Will Still Be Hot

> The affections are more reticent than the passions, and their expression more subtle.
>
> — E.M. Forster

Lacking strong family ties or obligations, many gay men have to depend heavily on friends for comfort and supportiveness. Yet many of us find it difficult to make deep, lasting friendships in the gay world.

"So many guys don't want to go to the trouble," a young friend of ours says. It's true that urban gay life is set up to provide a lot of socializing on a level that's simple and not very involving. Some gay men become so attuned to the tricking treadmill that their "friendships" seldom continue longer than their erotic interest in the "friend."

Another obstacle is that so many of us have spent much of our lives concealing our true selves from others. When we come out we discover that the gay world can have its cold, hard side, and we become so thickly wrapped in protective covering that it's difficult to reach others or to be reached by them.

Hardly unique to the gay world, though sadly common in it, is the man who is a great sponge for love. Soaking up every bit of affection that others can give, he's unable to return it. He tends to be overly possessive. His love life and social life are a desperate mixture of passions, disappointments, and rejections.

For some gay men, those who live in small towns or rural

areas, a busy gay social life is a beautiful dream, not a threat to deeper relationships. Their problem lies in finding other gays, not in dealing with them by the barful.

Where the friends are. The formula for friendship is no secret. In the ultra-familiar words of Emerson, ". . . the only way to have a friend is to be one." But it's hard to be a friend if one is in a situation that defeats the effort.

A friendship is enjoyed with a whole person, not just with plumbing and muscles and jaw lines. Standards that you may apply for a sex partner are likely to be excessively narrow, cruel and useless when applied to a friend.

The self-protecting man who puts a lot of barriers between himself and others may well panic when relating in terms of friendship, feeling that increasing nearness is a sign that his armor is coming apart. He has to be ready for this reaction and understand it as a false alarm.

The love-sponge may not readily identify himself as such, but anyone who notices that, time after time, he *exhausts* friendships should be suspicious of himself, and perhaps seek therapy to help him change his self-defeating mental habits.

Men who live in sparsely populated locales must make strong efforts to meet others like themselves. In these days of openness this isn't as hard as it used to be. An ad in a gay publication may well turn up a surprising number of other gay men in the same neck of the woods.

Many gay men, especially those who move to the boonies from cities, don't realize that there is almost always a local gay network. Quiet as it may be kept, "everybody knows everybody." All that's needed to plug into this circle is to meet one gay man or lesbian who has been living in the area for a while.

Straight men as friends

Once a gay man comes out, liberates himself, and perhaps moves from his hometown to one of the gay meccas, he may have no straight friends at all, especially no straight men friends. Considering the homophobia that many hetero males express and that virtually all openly gay men have to deal with, this is no surprise.

However, since the sixties, definitions of what constitutes

a Real Man have become far less rigid, so straight roles have become more varied. And with gay liberation bringing openly gay men into the workplace and social and political life, straights have had opportunities to experience gays as individual human beings, which is a good corrective for the ugly myths of locker room folklore.

Particularly among the younger generations, quite a few straight men have little or no difficulty relating with gay men. Whatever a hetero's age, it's a sign he possesses a certain maturity if his sexuality is not threatened by the existence of homosexuals. The rabidly homophobic man generally can't form close male friendships at all.

Once beyond the sex barrier, the potential for gay-straight friendships is very great. The gay man can have the pleasure of a close male friendship without the sexual tension or sexual competition that often lurks in the background of friendships with other gay men. The straight man, encouraged by our culture to view other hetero males as rivals for turf, power, and, most importantly, for possession of females, can relax with a gay friend.

Still, communication will not be perfect. The hetero may talk fairly frankly about his romantic life, but he is unlikely to want to hear a gay man talk of the same matters in any detail. A straight friend may not be comfortable in gay social scenes. While he might enjoy the novelty of a drag show, he may not care to be put in any situation where he himself is thought to be gay, such as a gay bar, where, additionally, he might have to deal with passes and gropes and gay repartee. Let's face it, the male equivalent of the woman who likes to hang around gay men is nonexistent.

But these are minor matters and may vary a good deal from man to man. The huge and gaping pitfall in a friendship with a hetero man is the temptation a gay man may feel to convert it into a sexual relationship. In this there is one simple rule to follow: *don't*.

Should the seduction succeed, and it may in a surprising number of cases, the friendship will never be the same. If the straight man does not end communication at once, he will be increasingly unavailable when the gay man proposes they get together. On occasions when they do meet, the hetero will be distant, on his guard. The friendship will crumble away. That seems to us a high price to pay for sex that almost certainly will be brief, uptight, and generally unsatisfactory.

A special situation arises when a long-time straight male friend's marriage crashes. Sure, it's okay to put him in your guest room for a few nights, until he can find new living quarters. And there's no harm in storing some of his things at your place.

However, the temptation to take him in indefinitely, creating some sort of odd couple relationship, is best resisted. True, your friend will be craving companionship, and he may even have forgotten how to sort his laundry – assuming he ever knew. It's easy to find yourself volunteering to fill in as a surrogate spouse, especially if the guy is attractive, and the chances are that he'll readily accept.

In time, however, his hetero male ego will recover from the trauma of the marital split. When this happens, he's apt to be ashamed of his former emotional vulnerability, of his need for help from another man, and a gay one at that. In the long run, your generosity may be repaid with resentment rather than with gratitude.

Straight women

As a female acquaintance of ours says, "With straight men I'm always Mother, Wife, or Whore. With gay men I can be just me." For whatever reasons, an appreciable number of straight women greatly enjoy the company of gay men. Most of them realize they are guests in a scene that is not theirs, and behave with discretion. However, the usual – and pejorative – nickname given such females is "fag hag" or "fruit fly."

That women do play a recognized role in gay male life, only to be given a put-down label, suggests a certain ambivalence about their presence.

Some gay men, a very few we believe, sincerely dislike females – period. In certain cases, scarred by bitter experiences in the family, a man may project his strong negative feelings about Mother on women in general. This may be the source of the passé fashion among gays of overtly disdaining females, which may in turn explain why blatant woman-haters today usually seem to be boozy old queens. Then there are those gay men who like females well enough, but resent their presence in gay bars.

As discussed earlier, gays appear to relate differently than straights to women from very early on in life. If some gay men display negative feelings toward women, many more show a distinct tendency to deify females. On Sunday, June 22, 1969, in gay bars all over the country, some patron came running in and shouted, in anguish, "Judy's dead!" Whereupon most of the other customers and staff broke into tears.

Among straight men the only female deities are sex goddesses. Free of this particular hangup, gay men respond to the female image and personality in other terms, and admire it for qualities which hetero men don't perceive. Our sense of Marilyn is different from theirs.

Female friends. A gay male can become very close with a straight woman because ostensibly neither is trying to put the make on the other. When sex is left out of the picture it's possible to develop a wide-ranging relationship in which each party can be comfortable. For the woman, the contrast to her encounters with straight men can be striking.

It's certainly not news these days that a good many heterosexual males treat females abominably. Until relatively recently most women have felt that they had little choice but to put up with this. But now there are increasing numbers of females who are unwilling to tolerate being treated as though they were inferior beings, intended only to wait upon males.

However, hetero male chauvinism is not fading graciously. A great many men make no bones about their rejection of the idea that they should deal with women as equals. It's not manly, not macho.

Exactly. Gay men can deal with women on an equal basis because we have nothing to fear. We don't have to prove anything to them sexually, and so they can't threaten our masculinity. As a result, the post-liberation female may find that the largest number of males who relate to her in an acceptable manner are gay. We can genuinely be *friends* with women.

Lesbians

Since we essentially have many of the same problems in

life, it's odd that gay men and lesbians don't always get on very well.

Partly, local custom may play a large part in this. In some areas gay men and lesbians simply have few chances to meet. The bar life in some cities is sexually quite segregated. The gay male social structure may be elaborate, and the lesbian equivalent slight or lacking.

And of course some gay men and gay women are doomed to relate badly to anybody of the opposite sex for reasons of personal psychology.

Finally, though gay people resent being stereotyped by straights, this doesn't always keep them from voicing generalizations about each other. "Dykes are so touchy/loud/aggressive." "Fags are so touchy/loud/silly." And so forth and so on.

This is an area where we might all try harder.

If as a gay man you feel lonely and have few or no worthwhile companions in life, you should ask yourself a few questions: Do you have your act reasonably together? Are you letting your sex life be your whole life? Are you severely limiting your chances of finding friends by ruling out whole groups of people?

Finding friends isn't always easy. It takes work both to discover and to keep them. But their worth is proverbially great, so if you find you have cast a few pearls, well, it's good to know just who the swine are. In the case of this particular gem, it's much better to give than to receive.

PLIGHTS AND PRESSURES

5 The Closet and Its Cases

Nature is often hidden; sometimes overcome; seldom extinguished.
— Francis Bacon

As gay men, most of us have spent a certain amount of our post-puberty existence struggling with the attraction we discover we feel for other men. This period of confusion and self-questioning almost always takes place in a closet with the door closed and locked from inside. Self-acceptance and self-definition precede coming out, and the process of defining oneself as gay may take a while, possibly years.

The time may be prolonged not only for personal reasons but also as a result of the influence of traditional psychology, which holds that sexual experimentation between adolescent males is a usual stage in a normal progression toward heterosexuality. But of course it's also a usual stage for the gay teenager in his progression toward homosexuality. All his friends go on from circle-jerks and the like to involvements with girls, but he, not yet aware that he is gay, impatiently wonders when *his* magical transformation will occur. He may wait and wonder into young adulthood.

Sooner or later, though – and in our society it seems to be getting sooner and sooner – the gay man realizes that adolescence is behind him and that, at whatever age, he is non-heterosexual. He faces the choice of coming out or remaining in the closet. That is, he either will accept himself as gay or pretend to the world, and possibly also to himself, that he is straight.

Like many major life decisions, the choice is rarely so clear-cut. In the process of coming out some men do a fair amount of waffling. Others, as the puzzle pieces all suddenly fit together, accept their self-discovery with relief. Those men who remain in the closet exhibit a variety in the syle of denial or rejection of their gayness.

What closet? A fair number of closeted men simply refuse to face up to being gay. They may or may not suspect the Awful Truth, but they are completely unable to accept it. Instead they suppress the sexual side of their existence. A retreat into celibacy is often accompanied by immersion in jobs, volunteer work, hobbies and the like. These men often achieve considerable success in the world. They're Freud's classic sublimators.

Should evasive maneuvers fail to keep sexual restlessness at bay, this type of man may seek a "cure" for his "problem" through some type of therapy. He may be fortunate enough to find a wise practitioner who will assist him in coming to terms with his essential gayness. However, many of these men select homophobic therapists, who can be extremely destructive to them.

Deep closet. Then there are the men who know in their hearts that they are gay but attempt to persuade themselves, usually quite ferociously, that they are heterosexual after all. This sort of man will seek to avoid any scene which might spark a homosexual yen, and he will display a strong interest in women.

If unmarried, he will feel the need to publicize his affairs to a boorish degree or to become an outright Don Juan. (The original, Juan Tassis, is thought to have been gay, by the way, but you're better off not mentioning this while visiting Spain.) Once married, this type is likely to father more children than anyone else on the block. Either way he stays busy trying to persuade himself that he really does like sex with females, or that he will, eventually, when he "really gets into it."

Something a lot of heterosexuals don't realize is that many, probably most, gay men *can* manage to have sex with females.

For some, there is a fair amount of pleasure in the act, and those who find it less than fun can create a desert-island situation for themselves, practicing a strict fidelity in thought and deed, with the wife or girlfriend as the only permissible sex object.

With the passage of time the deeply closeted gay man, whether intentionally or not, locks himself firmly into a heterosexual way of life. Friends and business associates will be straight and probably homophobic. He may take on financial obligations and accept positions of trust in the community. He destroys all alternatives, making life as a gay man appear impossible for him. He knows that discovery means ruin.

Convenience closet. Some closet cases operate in a far less rigid manner. They keep an active gay life going in one compartment, and in another they pass as straight. Once this sort of double life was almost universal among gay men who were not unduly troubled about their sexual outlook.

In recent years some gays, taking advantage of changing customs, have presented themselves as bisexual. Though many people believe the bisexual to be a mythical beast like the griffin or the unicorn, the truly bisexual male undoubtedly exists, but probably in smaller numbers than asserted.

A very young man who says he is bisexual probably is in the process of easing himself out of the closet and into gay life. An older man who defines himself as bisexual is likely to be trying to enjoy the pleasures of one way of life while he keeps the privileges of the other. On the surface he may appear less hung-up than other closet dwellers, but actually he's engaged in a difficult balancing act. After all, he does not want his standing in the swinging hot-tub scene to be jeopardized.

Marriage and the closet

We have no way of knowing how many men, knowing full well they are gay from skin to marrow, have chosen to marry women in order to appear heterosexual, but we believe the numbers are not few. And it's a fair guess that in most cases the wife is not aware of her spouse's true orientation.

It has to be said that gay men may marry for other reasons, too. A goodly number wed before they realize they are gay. As one of our friends said, "I had so many problems with physical illness when I was young, for years, that there was, so to speak, just no more room in my head for any other problems. Maybe my mind was acting self-protectively to keep my circuits from overloading. But when my life had gotten fairly calm and steady, after a year or so of marrige, well. . . ."

Some of us have a strong sense of dynasty, and feel that life is incomplete without procreating. Of course this notion can also serve as an excuse as well as a reason.

Sometimes sheer ambition calls the tune. There are signs of change here and there, but the corporate climb, and many others as well, can be difficult or impossible if a man has no presentable "little woman" at his side.

There's no way to know just how successful gay-straight marriages may be. No doubt many men have lived their whole lives deceiving everyone but themselves. It's safe to guess that the greater the element of theater, the greater the amount of stress, which is in addition to the usual strains common in any marriage.

Closet safety hazards

While playing it straight may give a man a sense of safety, life in the closet has many dangers, and discovery is only one of them.

Suppression and subversion of one's natural sexual impulses can lead to powerful reactions. Mr. Righteous Family Man may find himself suddenly and insanely in love with another male, possibly one who would exploit the situation. He could discover that his obsession is expensive to maintain, not above blackmail, or a cause of public scandal. Yes, it's Professor Unrat in *The Blue Angel* all over again. This time the irresistible Lola-Lola is a man, but his character may be equally frivolous.

For some men, living against the grain for a period of time can create stresses that eventually engender a variety of mental problems.

And there *is* discovery. The closeted man risks all every time he goes down on his knees in a public toilet, or camps it up a bit in the Pink Orchid Bar, or gets into some dramatic episode involving a hustler and a law officer or two.

More than his job, social standing, and personal life are at stake: if he is a father he has his children's well-being to consider. It appears more and more clear that nobody has the surefire formula for raising emotionally healthy offspring, but it's fair to guess that they do not benefit from an extra-stressful marriage, sex scandals involving Daddy, or the trauma of a divorce action brought by a broken-hearted or outraged wife.

The man who gets yanked from the closet into the newspaper columns may have to face it all without help from others. Even friends who can be counted on to feel a certain amount of sympathy might resent learning that they have been fooled all this time.

The gay man who lives a full double life, Mr. Straighto in the suburbs and Queenie in the bars, generally has an existence that, if more complicated, is less dangerous and less unhealthy. The gay world gives him a certain amount of useful information and, should his double life go crash, some refuge and support.

For example, not long ago an interstate highway rest stop, located between two population centers and notorious in the local gay world for tearoom action, began to be raided by the authorities. Over several weeks something like fifty men a day were arrested – almost every one married, a father, and respectably employed. Openly gay men in the vicinity had all heard about the raids, first by word of mouth and then via the gay newspapers. They stayed away. But the heavy closet cases knew nothing, so they continued to stop by after work for something quick, furtive, and anonymous. Thus the arrests continued, day after day.

Evil from the closet

Men who are playing straight not only pose a hazard to themselves, but also can be outright dangerous to openly gay males. We speak of the stone closet case. Almost inevitably he is extremely and openly homophobic to upfront gays and quick to blow the whistle on less closeted co-workers or acquaintances whom he discovers to be gay. He thereby increases his own feeling of security and makes a declaration of his heterosexuality by creating a we-they definition.

In a similar reaction to internal pressures it's not uncommon for the highly closeted man to become active in groups and causes which decidedly emphasize morality. In recent years this has been quite noticeable from time to time in various organizations of the New Right. Represented as a fight for All That's Good and True, homophobia is raised from defensive reaction to lofty principle: "We must protect the American family. . . ."

Usually without realizing it, the deeply closeted man may "come on" seductively with other males. Most of us have run across this sort of encounter at work or in a social setting. In fact, the scenario is pretty familiar: He's charming, maybe gorgeous as well, and he makes it clear that rather than dashing back to his wife out in suburbia he'd prefer to have a few drinks with you, maybe even dinner, depending on how his phone call home turns out. And he *does* prefer you, on a level of which he is only partly aware. As the evening continues you realize that you have picked up signals which were not intended to be sent. At best this situation can be frustrating and disappointing, and any attempt to lead it beyond the level of innocent, blind dalliance may lead to consequences ranging from acutely unpleasant to explosive.

Gay sex and the closet case

Even with hardline denizens of the closet, action *is* possible.

Alcohol, as everyone knows, is a terrific relaxer of inhibitions. Grass isn't too bad, either. Both have been used more than once to get buttons undone and zippers down. Alas, the effect is only temporary. Guilt replaces the magical glow and fires up denial mechanisms. Back into the closet he goes. And the booze (or pot) gets the blame. Why, he hasn't the faintest recollection of what happened, he says, and anything that did occur he will excuse with some variant of that famous and ancient line, "Boy, was I drunk last night."

The case who has brainwashed himself into thinking he really does like sex with women may take a different stance. Sex with a man can be rationalized as permissible as long as he maintains the masculine role, either using his partner as he would a woman or allowing him to suck cock and nothing more.

The crucial fact is that the man who is closeted almost

always is there because, on some level of his consciousness, he *wants* to be there. Horniness, it's true, may have its way and make him available, but not for long. If a man refuses to face his gayness, he will have strong denial mechanisms that propel him back into his refuge.

So it's possible to have sex with closet cases, but often it's a lot of trouble and sometimes dangerous. A lasting relationship, with or without sex, is rarely possible. For most men a scene with a heavy closet case is just not worth the trouble.

Closet case and upfront gay

Many gay men, particularly among the young and the politically active, believe strongly that everyone who is gay should come right out and say so, for the sake of unity and strength. Some of these people feel they have a duty to "expose" or "bring out" other men they know to be gay, in the name of progress and liberation for all of us.

As we see it, gay men are not the same person millions of times over, but are millions of individuals, each with his own life and each having to make his own decisions about how he wants to live it, however appalling his choices may appear to others.

Often when a man begins to deal with his gayness, he feels very alone. A level-headed gay friend who can be supportive and answer questions in a straightforward way will probably do more to effect an acceptance and consequent coming out than anyone who applies scorn or exposure.

Those who believe differently should think back to their own days of Facing the Fact. Can a man be expected to realize he is gay on Monday, come to terms with the discovery on Tuesday, and become openly gay on Wednesday? It may happen now and again, but it's hardly the common pattern.

Love with a case

The upfront gay man who lets himself become enamoured of a heavy-duty closet case usually is asking for a hard way to go. His closeted lover will want him to be invisible, may be afraid of letting the relationship develop "too far," could expect his self-assuring homophobia to be tolerated, and will refuse to circulate in the gay world for fear he "might be seen."

The best candidate for a relationship of the closet kind is the gay man who is living a double life. Either he will have an understanding wife, or he will know all the steambaths in town and be a master of the working-late-at-the-office ploy, the lunch hour quickie, and the frequent business trip.

Then there is the man who has married before realizing he is gay. If he takes a gay lover or fuck-buddy friend, it means he is in the process of coming out, and the partner should be prepared to deal with the following:

1. Lots of handholding, reassuring, and explaining about gay life;
2. Helping him through a separation or divorce;
3. Attending meetings of Gay Fathers with him;
4. Losing him or sharing him with several years of promiscuity.

The truth is, the best lover for a closet case is another of the same. They are working on the same wavelength, fear the same things, and can live with each other's self-deceptions. No doubt some have managed long-term relationships. But it's hard for two closeted men to meet, except in anonymous sex situations, where they will be unable or perhaps unwilling to communicate.

Hate from the closet

The other sort of relationship an openly gay man may have with a closet case is a wholly negative one. This is when, usually in a work or social situation, the case directs blatant homophobia towards the upfront gay.

What to do?

The openly gay man can be noble and ignore his jibes and cracks. Or he can return with a few remarks of his own, if he is good at that sort of thing. Or, in serious cases which justify playing it rough, maybe downright dirty, this is what the upfront gay man can do:

Get Mr. Closet off alone. Tell him you have his number, perhaps calling him "Mary" as you do. If you think it is probable that he circulates at all in the gay world, say that you have heard that he's been seen in some interesting places around town. And just as calmly, go on to explain that, being openly gay, any remarks *you* make on another man's sexual interests will be considered as coming from good authority. Then quietly suggest that he cool it with the bad-mouthing now and forever more.

A little chat of this sort can do wonders. Remember, calmness is all, and a sweet smile is a help.

We feel the Great American Gay Closet is not a healthy place in which to live, but we realize that some choose to dwell there, and that others feel they have no choice but to do so. Not everyone can agree with the brave words of Andre Gide, who wrote, "I would rather be hated for what I am than loved for what I am not."

The custom of the closet has weakened somewhat in recent years and it's to be hoped that it will decline further, assuming the gains of gay liberation continue. But for now, the closet remains one of the major, if not the most healthy or beautiful, fixtures of gay life.

PLIGHTS AND PRESSURES

6 Love Across the Line

> But what a mischievous devil Love is!
>
> — Samuel Butler

Love, like politics, can make for strange bedfellows. Back in 1948 a lot of folks were shocked indeed to learn from the Kinsey Report that about one out of every three American men interviewed admitted to having at least one adult homosexual experience. Many people find this hard to believe even today, but when the generalized homophobia that was current in the late forties is taken into account, along with an increasingly repressive social climate (Senator Joseph McCarthy's anti-red, anti-gay witch hunt was just around the corner), we suspect the statistics are on the conservative side: it's more than likely that some interviewees, even with the anonymity the Kinsey people guaranteed, would not admit to participation in homosexual acts.

Still, it's probable that only a minority of straight men in our society can be considered as potential sex partners for gay men. Some hetero males are so genuinely preoccupied with females that they don't even bother to acquire close male friends. Others are so homophobic that they're not about to go for any kind of male-male sex. (Some men become physically ill even thinking about it.) And many straights think of homosexuality as a disease, catchable by having sex with another man even once.

Men who don't feel threatened by the idea of getting it on

with other men are a minority among straights, but this is a big country, and in major population centers there are a fair number of them.

Who will and who won't, however, is hard to tell; it's an individual matter, basically. Some people feel that blue-collar males are more receptive to the idea of having sex with another man than are their middle-class and upper-class brethren, but at the same time are also extremely rigid in their notions of what's an okay sex act and what isn't.

In general, the straight man wants only certain kinds of sex with other men. To some extent this tends to reflect the homoerotic experiences he has had in adolescence, the "fooling around" that occurs at camp, in showers and locker rooms, and in other situations of close physical proximity with other boys. Displays of affection are extremely rare under these circumstances.

In addition, the straight man wants to keep his status as a heterosexual. Generally the sex will be done without kissy-huggy stuff, perhaps with clothes on, and with the gay partner in a role the straight man considers subservient. That is, a hetero will permit his cock to be sucked, and in most cases nothing more. A smaller number will engage in anal intercourse as the active partner, often with a good deal of enthusiasm.

A straight man will not suck cock or, worse yet, get fucked unless he is very experienced sexually and wildly curious, or perhaps extremely drunk or stoned.

Most straight men have an almost pathological fear of being passive in anal intercourse. They view it as the ultimate repulsive and degrading experience but, paradoxically, so seductive that a single encounter suffices to "turn you queer." Why this folklore is so tenacious is one of the mysteries of the heterosexual psyche.

For instance, in the novel *Deliverance* an episode of forced anal intercourse was used to add a sense of menace to what would otherwise have been a humdrum man-battles-nature yarn. The victim of the rape apparently suffered a permanent impairment of *machismo* and, back in the city, avoided the friends who had witnessed his humiliation.

This sort of overreaction probably stems from the hetero

male's relationship with the opposite sex. Women, the historically subservient and "inferior" group, get fucked; men do not. So the man who is passive anally is seen as something less than a man, some of his masculinity appropriated by the active partner.

This viewpoint is most obvious in situations where males are thrown together without women for long periods of time, as in prisons or on ships. In such settings some heterosexuals impose themselves on other men who are physically weaker or lower in status. Typically such relationships, though they may last for extended periods of time, are affectionless as well as demeaning.

At least a suggestion of inequality must be present for most straight men in any sexual scene with another male. It need not be spoken or acted out: the hetero can enjoy the power trip of getting another male to minister to his needs, who by so doing defines himself as less of a man.

Gays for straights

Some gay men markedly prefer sex with straight males, considering them to be "real men," not "faggots." This sort of man has to enjoy the role that the situation demands, which suggests that there is a good deal of gay self-hatred in his make-up, mixed with more than a touch of homophobia. When the pleasurable punishment of being coldly used and viewed with contempt isn't enough, it's always possible to approach the wrong man and get beaten up.

Other gay men consider sex with straights as a challenging recreation that calls on a number of skills. A friend of ours who is in this category and quite good at the game has given us these suggestions to pass along:

1. Expect some real hazards. It's necessary to cruise under very public and possibly very dangerous circumstances.
2. Be brazen when necessary. Signals obvious between gay men will probably go unnoticed by straights.
3. Don't bother with this hobby unless you're good at sizing up people quickly. Knowing when to hit on a straight is extremely important, so you have to be able to read him psychologically in a short time: Is he horny? That's the big question, followed by, How uptight is he?

4. Be ready to operate whenever lightning strikes. You might meet somebody on a bus or a street corner.

5. Improve your chances by hanging out where the straight men are. Our friend reports spectacular success at a park near his place, where he goes to watch recreation league softball games. He concludes that there's nothing like an afternoon of jocking around with the guys to bring out a hetero's latent yen for sex with another male.

If the scene is to be more than a toilet quickie – and many straights demand privacy – expect to use your place, not his.

Once he's in your house, the essential thing is to keep him from having time to reflect on the situation. First, keep him relaxed, and second, guard against any possible violent reaction from him. That is, quickly produce a drink, and then induce him to remove his clothes as quickly as possible, and before you remove yours. A man's vanity about his body, not always catered to by his wife or girlfriend, can be useful here. He may not only shed his role, the front he keeps up in public, but also a certain number of inhibitions, leaving him in a more experimental frame of mind with respect to sex.

After the fun is over Mr. Straighto will want to get the hell out as quickly as possible. He will not give his name or phone number, so give him yours if you think you'd like to see him again. The odds are great that he won't call, our friend says, but every once in a while. . . .

Servicemen. For gays who get off on straights, men in the armed forces comprise a special category. Usually they're young and full of sexual energy, away from the inhibitions of hometown and friends, and trying to have fun on very limited incomes. Many of them are aware of the longstanding if officially discouraged tradition of exchanging a little messing around with a gay man for such favors as room, board, booze, a night on the town.

The factors that make some servicemen easy pickups also constitute the danger in this activity. If they're young, they're likely to be strong. If they're away from the stabilizing influences of family and friends, they might become violent. Being poor, they may well follow up a punch-out with larceny.

Knowing where a "queer" lives, they might return with their buddies to give more trouble.

It's necessary, then, to be careful, but probably the majority of servicemen who follow this hallowed custom enjoy the sex. As a straight ex-army man told us, "Privates don't get laid on furlough. The nice girls want officers, and the other ones want money." And servicemen like to know someone who is at home in what is to them an unfamiliar locale.

A gay man who can come on as straight-appearing and as a pal is likely to make out best with servicemen. It doesn't hurt to be able to talk knowledgeably about sports.

Chances of love

It would be severely stretching it to elevate the majority of sexual relationships between gay and straight men to the level of love. Many a gay man has loved a man who, being straight, was unattainable or, at best, available only under the most limited and unequal of conditions.

Friendship is about the most that can be expected. After all, if a straight man fell in love with a gay man, then he would no longer be straight, except in extremely unusual circumstances of acute sexual liberation, and the gay man, preferring straights, might very well no longer love him back.

But our informative friend who likes hetero men has been quite adept at forming relationships which are basically not all that different from the gay fuck-buddy situation.

Sometimes the relationship can become deeper. This is especially the case with servicemen. It's not unknown for them to keep up a correspondence with their "pal" and to visit him after discharge from the service, sometimes with wife in tow.

Some gay men never go near straight men, sexually speaking. Others, for whatever reason, can't keep away from them. Men in the latter group must develop their skills and learn from a good deal of experience.

The fact that a good deal of gay-straight sexual activity goes on, quiet as it's kept, suggests to us that the line between heterosexual and homosexual is artificial, a construct. It may be better to think of the demarcation as a grey area and that the range of sexual response varies from person to person. Perhaps the full expression of sexuality, gay or straight or whatever, is curbed by taboo and custom; that is, by feelings of guilt and fears of exile.

WOMEN

"Gay men have manners, dress well, can carry on a conversation, they're charming. . . if only they liked sex with women." This was the lament of a lady friend of ours, and it suggests some of the anomalies of a relationship between a gay man and a straight woman.

As many of us are aware, hetero females have been known to fall in love with gay men. Often, where the man is openly gay, it's a case of a long-term friendship turning into amour.

After all, the parties to a close friendship between a gay man and a straight woman can never completely forget that they are a male and a female. As the friendship deepens, its shared intimacy can engender feelings that are distinctly romantic, especially in the female.

When love walks in, the gay man, if he is wise, will follow one of two routes – either go for it or put a stop to it. The third alternative, just letting matters drift along, is a recipe for disaster.

Where the gay man does not want the friendship to progress to something more intense, he may be able to bring his female friend back to earth by pointing out the obvious, which is that he is not willing or able to "convert." The problem here is that anyone falling in love sees the world through the famous rose-colored glasses: obvious obstacles are nothing and impossibilities are hardly anything.

Where sweet reason is no help, it may be advisable to avoid the lady's company for a goodly time.

Should a gay man fall for a woman, he would do well to ask himself a few questions:

1. Am I falling in love with love, loving her because she loves me; am I enjoying the situation rather than actually being in love?
2. Am I indulging a suppressed longing to play it straight, be the stud my dad wanted me to be, the husband and

father Mom would like so much?

3. Am I really gay? Could it be that I've just lacked confidence with women? (This is rare, but it does happen.)

The gay man who for the first time becomes romantically involved with a woman may find it quite different from any lover relationship he's had with other males. A woman is more apt to find it difficult to understand and accept tricking around on the side. She may want her man to cut off his relationships with other gay men and the gay world in general. She may want him to pass for straight.

For some men, weary of the emphasis on sex that's such a prominent part of the gay scene, and tired of what they see as superficial relationships, this can be a refreshing change. For others it's stifling, impossible to accept. A great deal depends on what a man wants out of life and how he feels about being gay. Most gay men will be able to cope so long as they realize that the relationship is sure to be different from the ones they are used to.

The disastrous course – neither becoming more deeply involved nor bringing things to a head – at first seems the easiest. It requires little effort just to go along, and it is nice to be admired and to enjoy the attentiveness and pleasant company. But sooner or later it's almost inevitable that love, not returned, will evolve into something perhaps equally passionate but a lot uglier. At best the woman will feel the man has been a tease. An ugly finale is almost inevitable, which means pain for two and a good friend lost.

We don't speak here of the gay man who is closeted, but of the gay man who is out. The closeted gay almost always, and usually very early on, gives a convincing appearance of having an involvement with the woman. It is the gay man who *hasn't* played such hetero games who can get into painful difficulties in relationships with women. However, the out gay male does have one advantage if he has to break with a woman. He can say that she is wonderful but that heterosexuality, charming as it may be, is just not his trip. This may be the least painful way to exit from a situation into which one has unwillingly or unknowingly drifted.

*

Lesbians

A loving couple made up of a lesbian and a gay man may occur, but for obvious reasons not very often. Of course, this has nothing to do with those well known marriages of convenience which have been fairly commonplace in the world of the theater and cinema.

Relationships with women may not be for every gay man, not even once, but some of us want the experience, or desire a variation from the usual, or have genuinely strong feelings for a certain female. The real problem is to avoid losing the values of friendship in the complex intensities of love. Frankness is rarely romantic or beautiful, but a relationship based on pretense, or a mass of false assumptions, or a dreamer's view of reality, has every chance of turning out to be extremely and needlessly injurious and painful. Whatever relationships one gets into, it's best to remember that there are two whole people involved, including two sets of very delicate feelings. Proceed with as much care as the situation dictates.

PLIGHTS AND PRESSURES

7 Life After AIDS

I know how men in exile feed on dreams of hope.
— Aeschylus

When AIDS-related diseases surfaced around 1980, and the realization grew that this mysterious, often fatal contagion favored healthy younger gay men, it suddenly appeared that the fast-lane gay lifestyle that had developed with gay liberation and the baby boom had a very high price on it. Something akin to panic swept the gay world in the United States. Many gay men chose to severely limit their sex lives, and business dropped off in steambaths and cruise bars.

With AIDS came not only great changes in gay life, but also the end of a beautiful reality – abundant gay sex in a delightful gay world.

We can look back and see the pretty dream forming, as reflected in the mass-appeal gay erotic fiction of twenty years ago. In Richard Amory's Loon trilogy (*Song of the Loon, Song of Aaron,* and *Listen, the Loon Sings*. . .), the secretive pre-Stonewall gay bar melts away, transformed into a huge forest, all pines and streams and clearings. And men. They're impossibly virile yet sensitive frontier types who sit around campfires to sing or recite rustic verses that would make Longfellow lose his lunch. These Ephraim McIvers and Cyrus Wheelwrights have sex and find true love with each other and with some of the most improbable Indians in all fiction.

The message comes through steadily: making love with men is beautiful, especially in a world where they can be open and relaxed about their desires. But the action takes place in a fantasy setting, with great openness in sex and minus bugs, bears, hetero men, or women of any kind. Loon-land is a "Wouldn't it be nice if..." kind of place, something that exists only in wishful thinking.

Came the sixties with its protest movements, hippies, widespread drug use, and, finally, Stonewall, and the urban gay scene popped out of the closet all over the country. This change can be seen in another gay trilogy, the Dirk Vanden "All" books (*I Want It All, All or Nothing, All Is Well*). These were published from 1969 to 1971. Vanden's message was that it was not only beautiful to make love with other men but that, aided by grass and acid, we can through sex reach paradise.

Of course plenty of gay men were having lots of sex before the late sixties, but the baby boom brought many more who felt that being liberated meant doing what you wanted and that doing what you wanted meant you were liberated.

Gay commerce accommodated and encouraged the new sexual freedom, and for many of us, especially the younger men, the bar-baths-drugs-disco-party route became a way of life.

Trouble in paradise. Rising national VD statistics gave the first warning of trouble ahead. (Of course changes in sexual morality among straights also had something to do with the increase in social disease.) Then, in the middle seventies it became clear that there was another problem: Internal parasitic infestations had risen to epidemic proportions among gay populations in American cities, reaching levels unknown outside of poverty-stricken third-world societies.

When it was suggested in the gay press that we might, albeit unwittingly, be undoing a century of public sanitation efforts in the United States, gay activists counterattacked fiercely. Neither they nor anyone else took these signs as warnings. That would be too much to expect: nobody stops a party because a couple of glasses get broken. Having a good time is very attractive, and sex is a powerful drive.

Then came AIDS. And panic followed, but this is a strong emotion and therefore doesn't last very long. In recent years business at baths has been rising toward pre-AIDS levels. Surveys in both gay and non-gay publications reveal that a substantial number of gay men have returned to their former recreational sex patterns.

Some men, especially those who are very young, feel they are impervious to harm. Others deny the obvious: "Really, I don't think one little orgy at the baths once a week could possibly be dangerous," or "I'm just too healthy to catch anything; I don't even get colds." Still others put their trust in magic. That is, they load up on masses of vitamins or consume mail-order concoctions in hopes of protecting themselves.

A few take a totally reckless attitude: "I'm going to die sooner or later, so I might as well fuck and party and snort all I can." For these men life is to be as it is in a porno novel, where sexually transmitted diseases don't exist. They're ignoring the reality of AIDS, which is the last thing in the world to make it go away. They are playing a form of Russian roulette with their own lives, and anyone who becomes infected, knowingly or not, and continues with promiscuous sex, becomes death itself for any number of other men.

These are all means, essentially, of denying the existence of AIDS. Very strange, yes, but when you stop to think about it, also very human. After all, we blithely disregard the possibility of death by multi-car collision on an expressway and the prospect of instant annihilation by nuclear holocaust, to name just two matters which would have left our ancestors unglued.

Facing it

Grim as it is, in an important sense AIDS scarcely deserves to be labeled an epidemic on the order of the Black Plague of the Middle Ages, or even the Spanish influenza of 1918. Unlike these pestilences, which swept much of the planet, it turns out that AIDS is not highly contagious. AIDS is not spread through the air or water, or by insect bites. You are essentially safe from it unless you engage in certain specific activities.

Unfortunately, this knowledge comes too late for those who already have contracted the disease. But now that science has determined with reasonable certainty *what* AIDS is and *how* it is transmitted, the rest of us again have the power to control our own destinies.

Perhaps we should think of AIDS statistics as something like homicide statistics: many people live out their lives in cities with high murder rates, yet never see a homicide, or even a violent crime. That's because they conduct their lives in such a way as to minimize hairy encounters – they stay out of high crime areas, avoid the wrong kind of people, and steer clear of criminal activities.

In terms of AIDS, avoiding hairy encounters means minimizing the risk of exposure, which means practicing what has come to be called safe sex. Basically this means that bodily fluids, particularly blood and semen, but also saliva, are not exchanged. Among practitioners of safe sex the condom, or rubber, once only a fetish item, is having quite a vogue, and not only for anal sex but also for the oral variety.

Urine is a bodily fluid, so watersports are highly suspect. Since AIDS may pass through cuts and wounds, fisting is avoided as a super high-risk activity. So is rimming: that's two-way exposure, like open-mouth kissing. Sex toys should not be shared. The wise man keeps them to himself. Like a clever gambler, he also plays the odds, not against them. The monogamous couple or a small group of trustworthy fuck-buddies who have sex only with one another reduce the chances very much.

Socially, the gay man who feels that safe sex is the only way to go these days will not bullshit about his activities, and will be wary of the sexual compulsive type and of the guy who says he's just back from Tibet or Tierra del Fuego, and hasn't made out with a single soul as yet.

AIDS and society

Syphilis, if legend is correct, was brought to Europe from the New World by the sailors on Columbus' ships. The 1918 "Spanish" influenza first appeared in an army camp in Kansas. AIDS first was identified in gay men. None of these diseases, of course, has confined itself to its original group. AIDS has appeared among heterosexuals who have picked it up sexually, not via hypodermic needles.

People like to be frightened, as shown by the popularity of roller coasters and horror movies, and people like to find scapegoats for their fears. AIDS already has excited a certain amount of extreme, irrational reaction here and there. Recent newspaper stories describe panicky rejections of AIDS patients by law enforcement officers and hospital employees, and even, in a few cases, of men losing their jobs merely for being gay.

Although homophobia is certainly an important factor in the public response to AIDS, there's more to it than that. Americans in particular have lost the ability to accept the idea that there is such a thing as an incurable contagious disease. We've forgotten that before the introduction of penicillin in the forties, many ailments that we think of as easily treatable were killers – including syphilis. And most of us are too young to remember the dreaded polio outbreaks which annually swept the country, causing closure of schools and other gathering places.

People managed to live with these horrors, mainly because they had no choice but to do so. Until science has conquered AIDS, this is the only rational attitude that we can take.

But whenever anything identified with gays is involved, a great many people are incapable of being rational. In some respects our supposed friends can be as dangerous as the outright homophobes. Liberals who are "tolerant" of homosexuality inevitably are in some degree homophobic. After all, it's not necessary to be "tolerant" of something unless you find it distasteful. AIDS has presented homophobes with a "respectable" rationale for limiting gay sexual freedom.

So it's to be expected that there will be mounting pressures to close the baths, police the parks, and lift the licenses of cruise bars. All this will be justified as necessary to protect society from the "wanton conduct" of gays.

It's impossible to tell the future, but should these reactions increase, they might become fixed in laws to segregate gay men and limit or forbid our activities. If we are not vigilant, we could end up where we were a quarter of a century ago.

Besides being careful about sex, we have to remain as levelheaded as we can about AIDS. We all know stories of men with AIDS deserted by lovers, evicted by roommates, and shunned by friends. Such needlessly fearful coldheartedness can only do harm: if *we* panic, then what can we say if the larger society reacts in a similar manner . . . against us? Obviously, it's in our best interests to help those who have AIDS, support efforts to find a cure or a vaccine, and remain as calm and reasonable as possible.

Every cloud...

So gay life is not a safe, woodsy existence full of gorgeous sex partners and flamingly uninhibited carryings-on. But the optimism apparent in the Amory and Vanden novels needn't give way to the gloom and fatalism of the old fifties-sixties "Twilight World" fictions, where, by convention, gay life and love had to end in tragedy.

If AIDS is a huge and very dark cloud, it just may have a hairline edge of silver lining. AIDS has brought the kind of life lived in the fast-lane gay world into question, or perhaps it has merely speeded up a process that had already begun. A certain disenchantment with the bar-bath-tricking existence had become apparent by the later seventies. Magazine and newspaper articles questioned the loss of humanistic values in favor of those of looks, youth, muscles, and the right clothes. Personals ads increasingly specified "non-bar type," "no dopers/boozers," "quiet homebody seeks same," and the like. Men spoke of being "boogied out" and of wanting other ways to live.

Many a gay man, of course, has hated to see the fun spoiled, but a good many others, forced to restructure their lives, have discovered much that's of interest that does not necessarily involve the incessant pursuit of sex. Some men find it a pleasure to relate with others on levels other than the purely sexual, and find they have gained in emotional depth. "I consider people's feelings now," one friend says, "which I didn't before, not really."

Whether AIDS will have a lastingly good effect on the gay world, along with all its bad ones, is impossible to say until the condition is banished and everyone is free to carry on as before. It's always possible that the narrow porno-paradise existence will take off again. On the other hand, AIDS may contribute in a major way to a redefinition of just what constitutes a liberated gay life.

We will see.

II
The New Gay World and You

8 Entertainment at Home

The truth is that men can have several sorts of pleasure.
— Proust

If there ever was an invention that appears ready-made for gay people, it's the video cassette recorder – VCR for short. A recent national survey showed that of about eighty-five million American households, slightly over a quarter had a VCR. In a contemporaneous survey by a national gay publication of its subscribers, nearly half owned a VCR.

Of course. We *do* like old movies, many of us. And it's fun to watch cuddled with a close friend or two. We can make comments that would get us shushed, at the very least, in a movie theater.

By keeping a sharp eye on the current TV listings, it's not hard to amass a large collection of favorite flicks off the tube, whether they be cinema classics, camp favorites, or just personal preferences. They can be recorded to keep, or just to see at some time more convenient than 4:30 a.m.

This means, essentially, that anyone with a VCR can create personally tailored television programming. For some of us this means no more cops-and-robbers series with car chases and beefcake actors. For others it means nothing but. We are free to choose what we want to see, when, and how often, and not be subject to the programming decisions of some TV mogul.

Nor do we always have to limit ourselves to family entertainment. *Citizen Kane, Casablanca, Rebecca of Sunnybrook Farm,* and *Our Miss Brooks* reruns have their charms, of course, but an informal canvass of friends and acquaintances suggests that the majority of gay men install their video cassette recorders in the bedroom.

When porno productions were exclusively on movie film, seeing them meant a darkened room, a projector, and a screen. The flicks were sometimes hard to buy, expensive when available, and easily damaged. By contrast, the video cassette is merely slipped into a slot in the VCR. It threads automatically and is viewed through the television set.

In the last few years more and more gay porn has become available on video cassettes. Many of the newer offerings, made expressly for the growing video market, are not filmed but taped, which gives them a greater sharpness of image.

The VCR and AIDS came into our lives at about the same time, and this no doubt partly accounts for the increasing popularity of porno productions aimed at the gay male consumer. A hot video is the companion of many a safe and solitary sex scene, and surely adds some spice to action between innumerable pairs of lovers.

But there is perhaps another and more subtle reason for the popularity of gay skinflicks. Unlike most other media, they depict gay men as desirable human beings – desirable for Just One Thing, maybe, and certainly never for any display of intellect or the more public talents, but still desirable. No comic stereotypes, no tortured souls, no social problems.

Sleaze and class. Much of the earlier porno and some of the current product is simply exploitive – poorly lighted, badly photographed, and featuring "models" (not "actors" – the definition of that word can only stretch so far) whose enthusiasm appears to be reserved for whatever drug they've been promised once the scene is shot.

However, the market has become more competitive, and the newer generation of gay sex flicks is marked by excellent technical values and gorgeous men. Most of them still can't act, but this may not always be their fault, since the dialogue, when there is any, usually sounds like this:

KIM: Hi, Hal. Come in. Say, you look like you have a great

body. Why don't you take off your clothes?

HAL: That's a good idea, Kim. But you will have to take off your clothes too, or else I will feel shy.

Old or new, many pornos accompany the action solely with music, usually some form of rock. Another advantage of the home VCR over the erotic movie theater is that the flick's sound can be tuned out, leaving the action to proceed in silence or to whatever accompaniment the viewer chooses.

If the market for gay porn has grown fairly large, it has not yet quite gone entirely legit. Titles, advertising, and promotion can be grossly misleading. Since the Federal Trade Commission is unlikely ever to interest itself in the problems of the gay porn flick customer, he has to be wary.

Information about porn films can be gathered from various sources. Some gay publications review sex movies, usually the ones playing in local theaters, but sometimes also new releases for the VCR market. The serious collector might do well to save these reviews as he comes across them, since they won't be available in the public libary.

It should be remembered, however, that this sort of reviewing is a nearly impossible job. Everyone is utterly loyal to his own sex fantasies, to what turns *him* on, so the same film full of surfer cuties may send one reviewer into outer space and set another one yawning.

Most of the better and newer productions are touted in four-page color announcements with pictures of the performers in action. Believe the photos; the words are usually pure, oldtime Hollywood hype.

At gay-oriented porno movie rental outlets, an excellent source of information may be the clerk who rents or sells you the cassettes. He'll know how popular your choice of movie is, and probably will have some idea of its contents and technical quality.

And of course there's word of mouth from friends.

So many tapes. . . Here are some rough rules of thumb for the newcomer who's faced with racks and racks of hot videos: Films set in New York City tend to display distinctly ethnic types. Many West Coast productions (notably those of William Higgins) feature boyish-looking young men, usually blonds and often with nearly hairless bodies. A wider variety of types and a greater range of young men appear in the offerings from Colt Studios and Bullet Videopac. Lots of muscles are usually in evidence, too.

The fan of S&M will find his tastes are rather neglected. While many porno films will show men dressed in leather gear, any heavy-duty action portrayed is almost sure to be simulated. Real S&M activities, perpetually in a legal twilight zone, are represented in only a few productions. When they can be found, they're often available only in poor to wretched copies. Some porno stores will not handle S&M cassettes. However, there is an underground of homemade works, sold and traded among private collectors.

Performers in porno movies are eighteen years of age or older, and while many of them look younger, none will ever be prepubescent. Whatever kiddie porn may exist is feloniously illegal.

Generally speaking, the older a skinflick is, the more likely it is to be poor stuff. There are exceptions, but even a good piece of work from the old days (*Bijou*, for instance) may have been so frequently or badly copied that it retains little of its original glory.

Selecting a VCR. The video cassette recorder works very simply, though it may take a few experiments to sort out exactly how to set up the timer. If you're not sure just how you feel about VCRs, you can rent one by way of introduction. Rental is not economical in the long run, however, and you should know that there is one tricky thing about buying a video cassette recorder. It's that there are two different types, the Beta and the VHS. A cassette that works on one will not work on the other.

You can get both porn and feature movies in either format, though currently there are more titles for VHS, which is somewhat more popular than Beta.

Most VCRs produce mono sound only. Stereo is now available in Beta and VHS, but at a significant markup in price, and except for some prerecorded movie sound tracks, there's not much programming in stereo just yet. But there's sure to be more soon, and stereo sound does add to enjoyment of a tape.

Getting tapes. Whether you buy or rent your favorite comedy, drama, or stroke film, and whether you shop in person or by mail, deal with the most reputable operator you can find. How long has this particular outfit been in business? That's a good indicator, and you can figure it out by how long it has been advertising.

Men who prefer to use mail order should check gay publications, both display ads and classifieds. The latter are especially helpful for specialty interests.

Rentals. Either by mail or at the store, a deposit will be required to insure return of the cassette in good condition. This is worked out in different ways. A very common arrangement is to give the store a deposit in the form of a completed credit card charge slip. You lose or wreck the tape, they put the charge through. Otherwise it's either returned to you or, if you wish, kept on file for future rentals. This is convenient because no cash is tied up, but some risk is involved: there have been instances of fly-by-night operators suddenly cashing in all the charge slips and leaving the vicinity at top speed.

Another arrangement is to require the tape renter to join a "club." A membership fee is usual, and part of it may serve as a deposit, alone or with a charge slip. Often a certain number of free or reduced-price rentals are a privilege of club membership.

A third way is for the renter to "purchase" a tape, with the understanding that he may exchange it later for another one, usually for a small additional charge. This arrangement goes on indefinitely. The disadvantage is that it calls for a significant and permanent cash outlay.

Video cassette rental stores are springing up everywhere, and even in the minority interest area of gay porn the competition is strong. It's a good idea to shop around for the best service for the least cost.

Commercial enterprises are not the only places to find tapes. In many cities public libraries have collections of video cassettes which can be borrowed by card holders. Of course they will have lots of film classics and documentaries, and nothing at all of the *Sex Slaves of Fire Island* kind of thing.

Copying with the VCR

With two compatible VCRs it's possible to copy anything you

record. Whole new worlds may open up. When you acquire a VCR, don't be surprised if several of your friends mention that they too are so equipped, and would you like to exchange an "interesting" movie sometime soon? Why, friends have even been known to join their recorders for duping sessions.

Copying is not difficult to do. You have to choose from several tape speeds, and the thing to remember here is that the faster the speed, the better the picture quality. The further removed from the original, the worse the copy gets, visually speaking, but the first couple of generations usually are pretty good. But a surprising number of rental cassettes have rather fuzzy images to begin with, so it's not always possible to get an acceptable copy. This can be a problem especially with porno films, where sharpness of anatomical detail is so important.

Some people still have collections of porno and other kinds of material on movie film. These can be copied onto video cassettes, but not at home. The necessary equipment is complex and expensive. Companies that do film-to-tape copying often run advertisements in gay publications.

To dupe or not to dupe. Copying can present both legal and ethical dilemmas. Thanks to the Supreme Court, you are free to tape anything you want off the air. As long as you keep the material at home for your own use, there's no problem. Just don't make commercial use of it.

This may not be the case with cable programming, but the courts have not yet gotten around to deciding what rules will be applicable to such cable services as Home Box Office. Of course many people with cable *do* record from it.

The legal situation is clearer with tapes you rent. In most cases it's illegal to make copies of them. The only exceptions are films not covered by copyright protection, which are old movies whose copyright has expired or been abandoned. Such films are in the public domain and can be copied or sold by anyone. Cassettes frequently bear notices to the effect that copying is not only unauthorized but also impossible because of some kind of electronic scrambler signal embedded in the tape. Could be, but, almost always, rental tapes copy just fine. . . .

Chances of getting caught making an illegal copy are laughably slight, unless you try to go into mass production and sales. But the effect of widespread copying is to reduce the cash flow back to the makers of the tape that's duped. While this may be no more than an irritation to large commercial companies, it can have a strongly adverse effect on smaller organizations. If porn movies are *too* widely ripped off, for instance, their producers might not be able to continue to bring us future epics.

Ready when you are, Mr. DeMille

Renting tapes made by others is all very well, but by teaming your VCR with a video camera, you can record anything ranging from parties to your own color productions. It's not nearly as difficult as it would be with movie film. Tape pictures are instantaneous; there's not the wait and certainly none of the legal problems you might have with processing by a film lab. And if the lighting is wrong, you can fix it, rewind the tape, and shoot the scene again. The video camera is light, easy to use, and records on the ordinary blank cassettes available in any video store.

While the basic camera is not very expensive, costs do go up with additional features. At present one of the more costly options is sound, but prices should come down as the technology is refined.

The video cassette recorder is particularly attractive to gay men because it caters to our interest in theater and film and other kinds of show business, because it enhances our sex lives in a vivid but perfectly safe manner, and because it allows us to be graphic, maybe even creative, in the video medium. Our guess is that the VCR is destined to be universally embraced throughout the gay world.

THE NEW GAY WORLD AND YOU

9 Correctly Political

> Those who expect to reap the blessings of freedom must, like men, undergo the fatigue of supporting it.
>
> — Thomas Paine

There are, as this is written, no fewer than three competing gay Democratic political organizations in San Francisco. Each club claims that it alone embodies the correct political stance for gay people. They issue often conflicting endorsements of policies and candidates. From time to time, officers of one club accuse those of another of wanting to further their own ambitions at the expense of legitimate gay concerns.

This sort of infighting is hardly restricted to San Francisco. Nationally, many gay men react to this sort of behavior by turning away from anything that smacks of politics. They don't see how it will help the cause of gay rights, and they don't see why gay politics has to be like this.

Gay men in politics say they dislike all the hassles too, but that they can't be blamed just because they had to split off from an organization whose leadership had been taken over by elements that were reactionary/irresponsible/radical/sexist, etc. As proof of *their* group's effectiveness, they point to the appointments to boards and commissions or to staffs of mainstream officeholders that they have received.

The San Francisco example admittedly may be a bit extreme. That city's sizable percentage of gay voters gives local gay political groups more weight to throw around. Moreover, in California, ever since the progressive reforms of the early 1900's, political parties in the eastern U.S. style hardly exist. This means that support by grassroots political groups is vital to victory at the ballot box.

San Francisco gay politics, though more exaggerated, are not really all that different from elsewhere. They clearly illustrate tendencies that pop up all too often in any kind of organized efforts involving gay people. Whether it's a float committee, an Imperial Court, a charity fundraiser, or a meeting to deal with some hot political issue, the odds are high that an ego-trip power struggle or a plain old bitchfight will erupt.

Often enough doctrinal differences merely express internal stresses engendered by a lot of members wanting a few powerful positions. The temptation is great for the dissatisfied to split off and form another club of their own. Now there are another set of offices to hold, and another set of prima donnas. But internal disunity will probably start up again, and inter-club competitiveness is almost inevitable. Both organizations will almost surely suffer in strength and effectiveness.

Geography makes no difference. It's as true in New York or Indianapolis or Atlanta as it is in San Francisco.

Listen to the speeches that are made at Gay Freedom Day celebrations anywhere in the country. Like as not you'll hear speakers putting down other gays as much or more than denouncing anti-gay elements in society.

In addition to squabbling among ourselves, gay men and lesbians are not noted for getting along well in politics. Thus the insistence on the formula "Gay *and* Lesbian" or "Lesbian *and* Gay."

Now hear this:

Out of all the pushing and shoving in gay politics has come a philosophy of sorts, identified by the catch-phrase "politically correct." The idea is to decide once and for all what's right and what's wrong and label it as "correct" or "incorrect." Now we have "correct" people, words, ideas, places, and things, and of course "incorrect" ones as well.

Even here there is no complete agreement; it depends on who's doing the defining. But these examples should give a fair idea of how the political correctness doctrine functions:

Consciousness-raising groups and political clubs are politically correct. So are Alcoholics Anonymous meetings, as long as the Deity is not discussed. Gays exploiting gays is generally regarded as incorrect, and few would disagree with that, except that the point is stretched to bizarre degrees: if exploiting is wrong, then gay businesses are wrong – especially gay bars, but also, it seems, any commercial enterprise that exists to provide a good time.

From one point of view gay neighborhoods are incorrect. They're seen as ghettos which are manifestations of oppression and self-hatred, as well as gay exploitation of gays. Others, feeling that the less truck with straights the better, extol separateness, gay jobs, gay businesses, and feel that nothing could be more correct than a gay neighborhood.

Both sides, however, agree that gay neighborhoods are correct for political rallies, leafletings, and fundraising efforts.

People easily become incorrect. Anyone who likes to live reasonably well is on the list, presumably because enjoying a decent meal and a good wine will distract one from attending meetings and rallies. Young white males are incorrect, just by happening to exist. They can become correct by acquiring a physical disability or by surviving to the age of sixty.

Sexism and racism are incorrect, as most people today would agree. But some people, taking political correctness very seriously, can carry their definitions rather far, suggesting it's sexist to write "gay and lesbian" rather than "lesbian and gay." Or suggesting that a man is a racist if he has had only others of his own race as sex partners, rather than choosing his tricks by some sort of quota system.

Curiously, one of the most incorrect things nowadays is sex. This strikes us as an odd point of view for a sexual minority, rather as if giants came out against tallness. But some activists berate gay men for having a supposedly unseemly preoccupation with sex, and they cast a cold eye on gay pornography, steam baths, and cruise bars. Porno, specifically, is considered incorrect because it's seen to be degrading to women. (That should let gay porn off the hook, unless women are degraded by their absence from it.)

If plain ordinary sex is viewed as incorrect, the kinky variety is a good deal more so. S&M is anathema.

The anti-sex outlook might appear to be a product of the

emergence of AIDS into our lives, but it's not. As a reading of gay publications dating from before 1980 will show, it was underway before AIDS, which only added to the agitation.

Words are declared politically incorrect, including some very familiar ones: "homosexual" is incorrect because it's a straight nineteenth century invention and rather too clinical. "Straight" is not correct at all, since it implies that gays are what straights are not, i.e., "twisted" or "warped." And "gay" is incorrect because it is said to come from centuries-old gutter slang meaning "whore" or "loose woman." And it suggests that homosexuals are frivolous by nature.

One of the oddities of the stance of political correctness is that it's often based on rather fanciful reasoning. The prevalent racism in our society, for instance, may well be reflected in a man's choice of sex partners, but on the other hand we don't have sex with persons we "should" have sex with, but with people who turn us on. Many gay men get it on across racial lines and have been doing so for a great long time, which suggests that, averaging it all out, there may be somewhat less racism in the gay world than in the larger society.

In the matter of incorrect words, things get very strange indeed. "Homosexual," for instance, was created because there was no neutral, descriptive noun. If rather textbooky, it's a great improvement over such epithets as "sodomite" or "bugger."

"Straight" comes from the expression "straight arrow," which, as those of us of a certain age are aware, came out of a weekly radio series of the early fifties that featured an impossibly brave and revoltingly perfect Native American by the name of Straight Arrow. So, "straight" as a synonym for "heterosexual" implies not moral purity but prudish stuffiness. And "straight" has long been used in contexts where it signifies difference, not superiority, as in theater parlance, where it harmlessly distinguishes a spoken play from a musical production. In any case, "straight," imperfect though it may be, is a great improvement over the term "normal," which was widely used as late as the 1950's even by gay people.

For all that's been written about it, just where "gay" came

from remains mysterious. In its specifically gay connotation, it appears to be less than a hundred years old, perhaps dating from the twenties, as one of the many code words then used to mean "homosexual." Unlike others, such as "so" ("Is he ... so?") and "advanced," the use of "gay" never died out, and went public with the advent of gay liberation.

Protesting the use of certain words strikes us as a true waste of time. These discussed above are commonly employed. Short of a reign of terror, there is no way to eradicate them from the language. This is particularly true with "gay." Should the word drop from general use in its homosexual denotations, which seems very unlikely, newspapers will keep it half-alive in headlines for years to come, like "ire" and "tot" and "tryst."

Just where does the rather curious and eccentric idea of "political correctness" come from? Perhaps it's to be expected when a largely individual and clandestine struggle such as gay liberation comes into the open and emerges as a movement: in the name of unity and preserving gains already achieved, demands for orthodoxy will be made.

The idea of making flat-out good/bad rulings about everything and everyone, a kind of brain-policing, has its chilling side, but to some extent it reflects the reaction of the politicized to the vast diversity of the gay world, to its built-in and sometimes immensely frustrating lack of unity. Add in the idealism of the very young politically oriented person: almost inevitably he feels that life could improve a great deal and very fast "if everyone would always __________" (fill in the blank). It takes most of us a while to accept the raggedness and asymmetry of the world.

Another element contributing to the notion of political correctness is embodied in the idea that sex is incorrect. To some extent this may stem from the variant of feminism that holds male sexuality to be automatically oppressive and threatening to women, but mostly it is rooted in a puritanism that comes from two sources. In its simplest expression – the feeling that if something is pleasurable it has to be bad and should be forbidden – puritanism has had a long if faltering reign in American life. But puritanism also seems to accompany revolutionary movements. Fidel Castro imprisoned homosexuals in an attempt to destroy Havana's gay life. The bloody persecution of gays in Khomeini's Iran has made world headlines.

Correct for what? What has the concept of political correctness helped us to achieve? As a Chicago newspaper publisher wrote, the 1981 San Francisco Gay Freedom Day observance marked "the official death of the gay movement and the birth of a movement that has absolutely nothing to do with gay," led by "'politically correct' individuals who revel in controlling gay movement events."

Yes, like-minded, "politically correct" people can take over gay organizations, but to what end? The presumption of absolute knowledge, the tone of moral superiority, and the hint of coercion impress a lot of people negatively, creating a hackles-up, "Who sez?" reaction. Which means dissension, splits, and resignations. In the long run, when the "politically correct" take over, less rather than more unity is the result.

Since the outlook is self-defeating, we suspect that "politically correct" will become no more than a quaint phrase, marking a certain early era in the history of gay liberation.

Gay power — how real?

The man who owns a Victorian house which he has painstakingly restored and the man without a job who's surviving on welfare payments may get it on famously in the sack for an hour, but their outlooks on such matters as taxes and governmental social programs are bound to vastly differ. Not only the ideological hazards we've pointed out, but also the social and economic divisions in the gay population must be confronted by the gay man active in politics.

Divisions of this sort were beginning to create trouble for Harvey Milk, the late San Francisco gay leader, in the months before he was assassinated in November of 1978. In his winning bid for election to the city's Board of Supervisors, a body second in importance only to the mayor's office itself, Milk had gained the support of organized labor. This was considered a coup: labor backing is highly important in San Francisco elections.

Along with labor, Milk wanted to forge a progressive coalition made up of not only gays but also the city's Latino and black minorities. These latter groups, however, felt that gays were taking a leading part in gentrification of their neighborhoods. If blacks and Latinos were threatened by this, many gays were disillusioned with the labor movement, having experienced homophobic discrimination from members and officials of various unions.

Worst of all, a sizable number of gays declined to ally themselves with Milk. (Echoes of this division continue today, reflected in the split among the city's Democratic clubs.)

Prospects for a grand coalition looked decidedly poor. Then a dinosauric state legislator from Southern California got an initiative measure onto the ballot. Had it become law, the state's school boards would have been required to search out and fire gay teachers.

Harvey Milk became a leader in the fight to defeat this initiative, touring the state to speak against it. The voters overwhelmingly defeated the proposal, and Milk was riding high, politically speaking. Tragically, barely five months later he was killed by a bitter and homophobic political opponent.

Where do we go from here?

In this bit of history there may be a clue as to how to avoid the all-too-common fate of gay rights measures in the hands of politicians and voters in this country. It also raises questions about the efficacy of working through one of the established national political parties, or of trying to form coalitions with other minorities.

Over the past several years voters have repeatedly tossed aside comprehensive gay civil rights laws in such diverse locales as Miami, San Jose, and the college towns of Lincoln, Boulder, and Palo Alto. In rare instances voters have upheld these anti-discrimination ordinances, but most existing laws of this type have never stood the test of the ballot box.

Contrast this discouraging picture with the results of the schoolteacher initiative in California, handily defeated by the voters. A *Los Angeles Times* survey more recently indicated that a majority of Americans nationwide — a bare majority — favor an end to job discrimination against gays, even though most of them disapprove of "the homosexual lifestyle."

This suggests to us that, in terms of goals to be reached

through the political process, it might be wisest not to go for the whole banana all at once. What, then are our priorities? That question is much too important to leave to the gay politicos, whose choices may be rather more personal.

Surely the first matter, essential to all future progress, has to be the abolition of anti-gay criminal laws that remain in force in a number of states. Until these statutes are eliminated, they can be used to keep gay people out of police forces, district attorneys' offices, and other public sector job positions. Insurance companies will continue to have an excuse to refuse to bond gay employees. Opponents of other gay rights legislation will have these laws to use as a "respectable" argument. Law enforcement agencies will continue to enjoy a legal basis for harassing gay establishments. Finally, but hardly least, gay people will continue to be prosecuted and imprisoned for acts which never should have been considered crimes at all.

Once the criminal statutes have been repealed, we can concentrate on the enactment of laws that protect our right to earn a living. These requirements can be difficult to enforce in individual cases, but they do have a very real effect over a period of time. Employers are forced onto the defensive, having to come up with a good reason for firing a gay employee. One lawsuit on this basis is usually enough.

Discrimination in hiring is tougher to get at, but in time it too can be expected to yield to the influence of this type of legislation.

Speaking candidly, we suspect it'll be tougher to get widespread legislation to insure gay access to housing and public accommodations. The majority of the American public, it appears, is not yet ready to believe that an obviously upfront gay couple has an absolute right to move into the apartment upstairs.

If the experience of other minorities is a reliable indication, and if having money means having political clout, then job integration needs to come first. Of course it's galling to have to wait before pressing for enactment of a law which would do no more than guarantee a right which we believe we should have anyway, but in the long run this may be the most effective arrangement.

We don't pretend that these goals cover all that needs to be accomplished, but they do constitute a solid, basic approach and a fair start.

How we get it

Since overt gay participation in the political process began only a few years ago, we don't have much collective wisdom about it. However, in deciding how to achieve our goals, two matters should always be kept in mind: first, we're a minority. Except in a handful of areas, chiefly urban settings with concentrations of gays, we are outnumbered. We can't win elections without help.

Second, our wide diversity means that, essentially, only civil rights issues, those bearing on our freedom to live our gay lifestyles, will bring out a specifically gay vote. On other ballot issues a bloc gay vote is unlikely to exist. And any gay politician who says differently is making a pledge that can't be fulfilled. This may look like a more serious drawback than it is. Issues that unite us lie in a narrow range, but there our feelings tend to run deep. Therefore, we find it easy to make common cause with other opponents of a candidate hostile to gay rights. In this narrow focus we have an advantage over such groups as the Moral Majority, which spreads itself thin dealing with matters ranging from public school prayer and sex education to abortion and creationism.

As a minority, perhaps ten percent of the electorate, we are often pivotal in deciding elections and ballot issues. The question is, just what is the best way to exercise this leverage in the political arena?

Many gays answer that we as a group should align ourselves with one of the mainstream political parties, arguing that in this way we become part of the coalition of groups on which the party depends to win elections. In return we can expect the party to be receptive to our needs and to champion issues important to us.

The theory sounds good and is endorsed by a number of gay political leaders. However, since close elections are decided by voters with no firm attachment to any political party, candidates and parties tend to concentrate on wooing these unaffiliated voters.

Consider the political history of another American minority: from Reconstruction days up to the Great Depression of the 1930s, most blacks who were able to vote cast their ballots for the Republican party. In return for their loyalty they received precious little. The situation reversed in Franklin Roosevelt's time, when the black vote came to be regarded as the property of the Democrats. However, in recent years complaints have been increasing to the effect that the party is ignoring the needs of blacks.

The diversity of gay people makes it very unlikely that a decisive majority of us will permanently affiliate with any single political party. But this may be an advantage, making us voters who must be specifically wooed and won, if only on a certain few issues.

The religious right. In spite of the fuss that it has been making in recent years, we doubt that the religious right wing in the United States is any bigger, relative to the entire population, than it was thirty years ago. Those who are awed by its apparent vigor are likely to be basing their estimates on recollections of the 1960s, when adherents of conservative religious doctrines were in disarray. Then an unpopular war was undermining their simplistic patriotism, while at home their traditional beliefs regarding the social order were being overturned by governmental decree.

To appreciate why gays have now become a major target of the religious right, it's important to remember that this group historically was overwhelmingly segregationist, having its strongest base in the states of the old Confederacy. The fundamentalist right embraces a religious doctrine which depends strongly for its appeal on a "we-they" view of the world, no doubt because so many of its adherents have represented less highly educated, less economically powerful sectors of American society.

After court decisions and civil rights legislation had made it impossible for the fundamentalist right to discriminate overtly against ethnic and religious minorities, it took a while for "safe" new objects suitable for the scorn of the faithful to emerge. For the right-wing preachers, gay liberation, like women's liberation, was a godsend.

Hatred of gays, along with hatred of abortionists and of "fem libbers," meets a fundamental need of the religious right. Being based on a good guys–bad guys mentality, these faiths are fueled by hatred as much as by love. It is therefore futile to imagine that arguments over the meaning of passages in scripture, or any other sort of logical reasoning, will change this group's implacable hostility toward gays.

Still, it would be a mistake to consider the religious right the wave of the future. True, it will continue to pose a danger to us, and in those regions where it is numerically predominant it will hinder local legislative progress in the direction of gay rights. And in recent years it has been given an appearance of increased credibility on the national scene by expressions of support from a popular president. But neither church membership figures nor opinion polls confirm that the American populace is shifting toward religious fundamentalism. The religious extremists are vastly outnumbered by our potential friends. It is their apathy which must be our target.

Your role in gay politics

The gay man who wants to be politically active will have to find a gay political club in his locale that's suitable, from his political point of view. If there isn't one, the alternative is to join a mainstream political organization.

Either way, here's what to expect: if an election is coming up, a new member will be welcomed with open arms, because there's work to be done. It won't be anything glamorous, more the door-to-door canvassing, telephone soliciting, envelope stuffing kind of thing.

The fun stuff, like press conferences, speech making, and meetings with the mayor, is done by the club's officers. Usually they have been around the longest, perhaps since the club's beginnings, and they like to stay in control. Generally speaking, any ideas a new member would like to express should wait a while, until he has paid his dues by volunteering for a sufficient number of distasteful tasks.

Anyone who joins a gay club in the lull between elections or other political battles may be viewed as some kind of interloper. But perseverance pays off, and by the time of the next election you will have seniority over the fresh recruits.

How does a gay political club function? Typically, the organization holds periodic general membership meetings where decisions are made regarding club leadership and policies. The newcomer will very likely observe that a great deal of influence can be wielded by a determined minority of members. They can propose amendments to a pending motion one after another, until the general membership hasn't the foggiest notion of what is being considered. The proposal may thus end up derailed, sent back to a committee for study.

Another classic device is "come early, stay late." The meeting is made to drag on and on, with floor speeches, points of order, requests that the speakers yield, and objections. The fainthearted, the easily bored, the time-pressed, and those with delicate rear ends will depart. And the minority becomes the majority.

The intrigues and carryings-on of political groups may put off the prospective member, but no less august a body than the United States Senate operates in exactly this fashion.

Some simple preparation will enable anybody to function effectively at political meetings. Supposedly the proceedings are governed by Robert's Rules of Order, but it's probable that nobody present will actually have read them. Oh, one or several members will consider themselves experts on the Rules, but almost always the truth is that everyone is winging it, depending on what they can recall from school days. *Robert's Rules of Order,* by Henry Martyn Robert, is a slim volume, easily understood, and available in any public library. The man who takes the trouble to study it will be in a position to run circles around the other club members, once the maneuvering begins.

Gay politics may have its extremes, its star-trippers, and its silly side, but we are new to the political arena and, since much knowledge is gained only by experience, we have to expect some growing pains. The desire of many gay politicos for a solid, all-encompassing gay unity may be unrealistic, but it does express the seriousness with which many of us take political matters.

Politics is serious indeed, one of the most vital concerns for us as gay people. How easy and comforting to think that our recently gained freedoms can be taken for granted, to tell ourselves that we can only progress, never go backward. History, however, informs us differently. Until quite recently the greatest freedom gay people enjoyed in modern times was had in Germany during the nineteen-twenties. All of it was swept away by the outcome of a single election.

The United States today is not the Germany of 1932, but gains can still be lost. Compare a random selection of current gay publications against their counterparts from the middle 1970s. You'll notice that both editorial contents and advertisements were noticeably less inhibited back then than they are today. Clearly, the lid has been pressed back down to an observable degree.

So it is true that we ignore the political process very much at our peril. We must participate if we are to keep, much less increase, our freedom. Not every man will be interested in joining a political organization, but there are all the other things one can do, and everything helps: letters to office holders and editors of publications, calls to radio talk shows, financial donations in support of your beliefs, and, of course, the vote.

Many feel that none of this really helps very much. The problem is that it's difficult to always know just what effect an effort may have. However, what we have done so far has in many cases bettered our situation. Contrast our current lot, imperfect as it may be, with the lives we had to lead a quarter of a century ago, when gay rights organizations hardly existed and gay unity of any kind was the most impossible of dreams.

10 Making a Gay Buck

> We work not only to produce but to give value to time.
> — Delacroix

A blessed few of us can clip our coupons, count our bonds, and wonder idly just *how* to get through another leisure-filled day. A certain number of us, young, gorgeous, and amiable, have the bills paid by "Daddy." But most of us have to earn a living. Even men who have no financial need to work often will anyway, just to have something to do, or to feel useful, or to make even more money. And many young men who have been kept, or could be, are well aware that it only *looks* like it's not hard work.

Gay men can find problems in the workplace, ranging from denial of advancement to outright homophobic harassment. In reaction, if surveys are to be believed, many of us respond to job discrimination in the classic fashion of upwardly mobile minorities – by being high achievers. The statistics are not terribly reliable, partly because it's often difficult to identify members of our group, and partly because most applicable studies have been commissioned for commercial purposes and are not exactly disinterested. However, given the job insecurity that being gay may bring, it's only logical that a man might react by being damned well qualified for his work and good at performing it.

This widespread compulsion to excel is very likely the

source of two prevalent myths about gay men. One is that we are more creative and talented than our heterosexual peers. The other is that we are all involved in secret groups that plot to help other gays while denying heterosexuals in the same field the opportunity to compete on equal terms – "the Homintern." Being more talented and in ruthless cahoots with one another, we are disproportionately represented in the arts – or so the beliefs go.

While it would be nice to believe that merely by being gay we are automatically in some way superior to other people, the facts don't support this notion. To function well in any of the arts requires a lot of exposure to the form, perhaps from childhood, and young gays often do immerse themselves in artistic pursuits as a retreat from an environment they don't fit into. It also requires a lot of time, which gays frequently have, not having to deal with marriage and children as a rule. And it requires a lot of hard work, which brings out the gay compulsion to excel, once again. Since the arts, socially, are known for accepting a wide range of people, they have served as a refuge for gays who may have found life very tough in the mundane world.

As for gays forming cabals to help each other and squeeze out everybody else, most of us know what rubbish that is. While gay may favor gay sometimes, a pattern visible among other minorities and quite common with the straight majority, it's hardly inevitable. A play director who's gay, given the choice between a lousy gay actor and a good hetero actor for a role, is bound to choose the latter. Otherwise he'd be jeopardizing both the play and his future career.

The fact seems to be that gays are not only as fierce in competition with one another as they are with heteros, but sometimes appear especially to relish cutting the professional throat of another gay. This may be particularly the case where one man is closeted and the other is open about his gayness.

Although a lot of gay men like to believe the notion that we are especially endowed with creativity, in truth this belittles the hard work most talented gay men have put into their accomplishments, surmounting both the strains that can accompany being gay and the difficulties imposed by the world.

Indeed, a high proportion of gay men are workaholics. Many combine this with playing hard as well, which adds up to a good way to undermine one's health. A man should engage in an occasional stock-taking and ask himself just what his goals are, where he really wants to be in five years or ten.

The gay man who is working his ass off mainly to win the approval of the straight world is not apt to be getting any real satisfaction for himself. Like anyone dissatisfied with his job, he should think hard about moving on.

I want out!

Among the several alternatives to the mainstream job arena is gay commerce. Since gay businesses, although much on the increase in recent years, are not that numerous and usually classifiable as small enterprises, they offer a limited number of jobs, and many of them are not very lucrative. Therefore, most gay men who want to get into gay commerce think in terms of going into business for themselves. In fact, it seems that almost every gay man sooner or later finds the idea of his own gay enterprise irresistible, at least until the morning comes and it's seen as a lovely fantasy, doomed to fade away. But there are those few who decide to make the dream a profitable reality. Very often they are lovers or close friends who plan to triumph together.

They should realize, before getting carried away, that starting a business is never easy, and that gay men face some unique problems in the world of commerce.

First, starting up a business can be a sure-fire route to hassles with straights. Most enterprises, but especially those involving food or alcoholic beverages, will require a great tangle of licenses, permits, and inspections. This means extensive dealings with non-gay people; by the law of averages a certain number of them are bound to be homophobic. Suppose the area where you want to open a bar has a dozen other cocktail lounges. Maybe not a one of them meets the specifications regarding fire exits. But, as a gay entrepreneur, you can be sure *your* bar will be required to do so.

This pattern could continue well beyond the licensing stage. Loading zones may be available for customers of neighboring businesses to park their cars in, while patrons of your place get tickets. Zoning violations will certainly be the basis for a complaint by *somebody.*

Then there is the possibility of extralegal harassment, such as rocks fired through plate glass windows.

These sorts of problems do increase the overhead, but they're not inevitable. Attitudes vary from place to place, and a gay business with a low profile may not face anything like the difficulties something more upfront would encounter. Of course in recent years gay neighborhoods have developed, and there the problems may be less. But competition can be more fierce if the market basically is only gay men, and rents may be higher than for an equivalent facility in a non-gay neighborhood.

The bottom line. Gay enterprises are not immune to the hazards common to any new business. The horrendous failure rate is well known, so our prospective business moguls would be wise to consider some of the whys.

A major cause for a business to wither and die is the owner's unfamiliarity with its requirements. A man may be able to produce splendid sit-down dinners for twelve at home, but that's no guarantee he can come up with comparable results under restaurant conditions. A florist shop may be charming as an idea, but it won't be a reality for long without a thorough knowledge of wholesale and retail flower marketing.

Another route to disaster is lack of capital. It's a rare business that manages to break even within the first year of its existence, much less turn a profit. In fact, a more realistic period to expect to wait before the ink stays nice and black is three years. If startup costs are to be met by income from another job, a man has to consider whether he can keep his health and sanity while working eighty or more hours a week.

Misjudging the market is another big reason why businesses go broke. A friend of ours finally realized the dream of his life, to own a gay bar. He created exactly the sort of drinking spot *he* had always wanted to be able to go to. And beautiful it was. Unfortunately, the bar's ambience held small appeal for the guys in the provincial city where it was located. They continued to patronize the downtown dump and the barnlike disco out among the used car lots on the edge of town, and our friend went broke.

A related matter is possible oversaturation of the market. When someone asked a restaurateur friend, "Just how many French restaurants is this burg gonna end up having?" his answer was, "Exactly one more than it can support."

Location can have a great effect on a business, of course, and many a shop or service *has* gone under because it was in the wrong place, though not so often as disappointed proprietors claim.

Not long ago we dropped off a friend at his bank. Because of the street configurations and a one-way traffic pattern, we could approach the institution only by a roundabout route. The bank is doing fine there, but a business which depended heavily on customer access by automobile wouldn't have a chance.

This brings up another possibly fatal difficulty for the new business – parking. Its availability and importance have to be closely considered in terms of relevance to the planned business. Such institutions as schools and athletic facilities in the vicinity can have devastating impacts on a neighborhood's supply of parking spaces.

Something many an unsuccessful entrepreneur doesn't want to admit to is plain old sloppy business practices. The man who is impatient with details and regards bookkeeping as an intolerable bore, who never gets around to the paperwork, may show up at his shop one day to find the tax authorities have padlocked the door.

And as long as a business appears to be thriving, credit for goods or raw materials is not difficult to get, as a rule. But once a few checks have bounced, however innocently, suppliers are going to want to be paid for past goods and will demand cash for everything from now on. Few businesses have sufficient resources to continue operation on this basis.

Minority of minorities. The entrepreneur who looks to a mainly or exclusively gay clientele for his customers may unwittingly limit his market to a relatively few members of the gay community. Tastes vary so much among gays that it is easy to end up appealing only to a minority of what is a minority to start with.

This is especially true in the bar business. Though many

customers don't realize it, most gay bars are "orchestrated" to attract certain customers and disinterest all others. Music, for instance, brings one kind of crowd if it's country-western, another if it's rock, younger men if it is loud, older if it is background noise. Seating makes a difference, too. Gay men like to sit on bar stools up at bars, and they like to stand and pose. Lesbians tend to prefer to sit at tables or in booths, and they are not much for standing about.

And on and on.

The bar that is the chic, hot place To Be Seen may be crowded for six months or so, then be empty every night, deserted as "nowhere" by the fashion-conscious crowd that's moved on to a newer, hotter place To Be Seen. Some of these bars that look like they're taking in money by the bucketful are actually going broke. The customers crowd in, but then order just one drink, spending their time admiring and being admired.

Restaurants pose difficulties similar to bars. Too limited a menu means loss of a lot of customers. This may be no problem if the eating place attracts a straight as well as gay clientele. Otherwise. . . .

Considering overhead, competition, and distribution problems, anyone these days who goes into the bookstore business, and particularly the gay bookstore business, must be a little crazed or else incredibly brave and determined. But either way, good for him. Gay or not, a bookstore has to try to satisfy a wide variety of tastes, or else take a big chance and specialize in one area of interest. Some booksellers do both, offering a general stock and also specializing in one field, like Armenian history, say.

Any bookstore has to be located in a space that's large enough to allow lots of display and lots of storage. Strictly gay bookstores have given the appearance of stability over the last twenty years or so, but by now almost every large city in the country already has at least one, and in smaller urban areas the demand may not be sufficient to keep such a business going. A good deal of gay book sales from established stores is by mail order, so almost every one of them publishes one or more catalogs every year. This can be a labor of love or a damned nuisance, and it certainly adds to the overhead, but many gay book readers live in remote areas or, alas, still want to buy their gay lit anonymously, in plain brown wrappers.

Proceeding with vigor

If all this hasn't scared you off, and you still want to go into a gay business for yourself, you will of course prepare to be expert in your field. Lots of books give advice on starting up a business, but here are some particular concerns for gay enterprises which are not likely to be discussed in the titles you can get at the library:

1. If you'll be renting the business premises, which is usually the case, go over the lease very carefully. Note especially the renewal provisions. A landlord who discovers a business is gay, or who decides he doesn't want such an operation on his property after all, can refuse to renew unless the lease provides otherwise. Or he could take advantage by jacking up the rent outrageously when the lease expires.

2. Do your homework. Pay for studies of foot traffic or gay bar patronage or whatever, if you haven't the time or expertise to do them yourself. Use professional consultants if necessary. A fee can be a good investment, and in any case it's tax deductible.

3. Talk with other people in the same business that you want to start up. Often, unless you will be providing direct cut-throat competition, they may be very helpful. And if it seems they all want out of the business, maybe go so far as to offer to sell you theirs, then think twice about getting into this particular line of endeavor.

4. Be leery of purchasing an existing business. This is especially true if talents and personalities make the enterprise go. How do you know the great cook who's been there for years won't quit when you take over the restaurant?

If you do buy an existing business, especially if it is your first time out, be sure to get a written agreement from the former owners, one that prevents them from going right back into the same business, maybe across the street, in direct competition with you. Have a lawyer draft this, so it'll be sure to stick.

5. Expect to have some hassles, and get the proper professional assistance. Do this early on. You'll need an accountant from the start, to set up your bookkeeping system and attend

to such things as depreciation schedules for the equipment you buy. Do not wait until the business has been operating for six months; by then it may be too late. And as we have pointed out, you will need a lawyer as early as the lease negotiations.

6. Be consistent in running your operation. Know what image you want the business to have, and what segment of the community, gay or whatever, it's intended to attract. Casual hours and sometimes-available goods and on-again, off-again services are a sure way to discourage repeat customers.

7. Expect to invest a *lot* of time and effort, not to mention money, in your business. Enterprises do not run themselves, even after they're started, successful, and going nicely. It's a big mistake to play the Grand Seigneur and leave the actual running of the operation to others. Employees are not getting what you are out of the business – even if it's only your pride of ownership – so they do not have the same feelings about it that you do.

Adios, rat race

Between the wage slavery in the straight world and the rigors of running one's own gay business, there is the middle road of investments. Whatever else can be said about them, they are completely lacking in homophobia. A gay man's certificate of deposit pays the same rate of return as anybody else's. Real estate appreciates regardless of anybody's sexual preference. Tenants can't refuse to pay their rent if they find out their landlord is gay.

The only problem is, a lot of us aren't in a position to invest, or at least we think we're not. But we could be mistaken.

It's often possible to make investments without putting extra strains on our wallets. For instance, we must have a place to live, but this doesn't mean we necessarily have to pay rent for it. After the tax advantages of property ownership have been taken into account, the monthly payments may not amount to much more than the rent check. And as the property increases in value, so does the investment.

Probably more gay men have gained the freedom to live their lives as they please by means of careful investments than by owning their own business. This is a good thing because not all of us are temperamentally suited for business. Saving

THE NEW GAY WORLD AND YOU

11 Up, Up and Away!

Afoot and lighthearted I take to the open road.
— Walt Whitman

For the gay man the pleasures of travel can be complicated by two problem areas that sometimes overlap. We speak of facing homophobia and finding action. These can differ greatly from place to place, but a basic differentiation can be made between travel problems in the United States and out of it.

In this country, assuming you don't wear a feather boa while strolling at high noon down the main drag of Nadaville in black patent leather sling pumps, there are two small matters to consider.

The first is having tricks in your hotel or motel room, perhaps overnight. Basically, if you have paid for only one person to use the room, then the establishment has the legal right to bar non-paying occupants. However, the house detective — classic snoop of movies, books, and dirty jokes — is not likely nowadays to care much about "immoral" activities of guests. You don't have to concern yourself with any official peeking through your keyhole.

As a practical matter, management is unlikely to be concerned with your visitor if he can pass for a relative or a friend, stopping by for a reunion and a nightcap. An obvious hustler, on the other hand, might well be noticed. (That's why professional gents who work the better hotels affect the preppie or young executive look.)

Management will probably pay no attention at all if you and your new acquantance get together in the afternoon. Suspicions arise along with the moon.

The other problem involves travel with a lover. In the olden days it was unmarried heterosexual couples who had to resort to the "Mr. & Mrs. Smith" ploy to check into a room together. And nothing was thought of two persons of the same sex sharing a room. But not a bed, of course. Today it's easy enough to book a room with a double bed, for two men, and it's possible no eyebrows will rise. But still, we continue to hear tales of the snotty room clerk – often a closet case of the ultra-transparent variety – who confronts the gay couple with "*Obviously*, there's been some mis*take*. . . ."

Traditionally, many gay lovers when traveling request a room with separate beds. The trouble is, the amorous couple can end up with two very narrow singles. The trick is to ask for what in the hotel/motel business is called a "double double." That is, a room containing two double beds. Strangely enough, this doesn't always increase the room rate, since it has become a fairly standard arrangement in many of the newer plastic motels that have sprung up along the interstates.

Travelers who say to hell with 'em can, in places where private gay sex is legal, insist on a room with one double bed. The sprawling modern motel, with its registration desk perhaps a quarter-mile from some of its rooms, gives one the opportunity to be both discreet and dishonest at the same time. One of the pair registers at the motel desk while the other waits in the car. If the stay is of one night's duration, probably not even the maid will be the wiser.

Gay hotels. Difficulties with homophobia and getting some action can be eliminated by patronizing the growing number of hotels and resorts which cater specifically to a gay clientele. Most are found in the United States, but there are some abroad. The gay hostelry or spa can present problems of its own, however. Many of them, including some that are heavily advertised, are located in extremely crummy neighborhoods, some so bad that you put your life on the line every time you step out the door. In country settings the charming resort may be virtually a fortress of gaiety in a land of homophobes. The effect can be claustrophobic, and if the resort isn't all it's advertised to be, it can be intolerable. Two weeks with bad food and a mob of obnoxious bores isn't the greatest possible vacation.

Assuming you are unfamiliar with a city, you can be reasonably sure of finding a gay hotel in a good location by checking with a friend who is familiar with the area. Otherwise it might be better to book through a gay travel agency, making it clear that you don't care to vacation in switchblade territory.

You can insure against a bad time at a resort by doing two things. First, don't believe every word of the glowing brochure. Second, do some research. Is this place near some other gay resorts? Is there a town nearby with a gay bar or restaurant or two? Such information will give you an idea of just how remote the resort is and just what options you have should you find the Sunnydale Lodge crowd uncongenial.

Foreign countries

One can be openly gay with little or no trouble in much of Western Europe. Most of the world, however, is very much pre-Stonewall in attitude toward homosexuality. That is, pretense, furtiveness, and hypocrisy are the rule. Discretion is the best policy. After all, the gay man from the United States is traveling not only through space but also in time. Wherever he goes, almost, it's likely to be into what is, for him, the gay past.

Many Americans feel that somehow the Constitution and the Bill of Rights travel with them wherever they go, which is most assuredly not the case. Keeping this in mind may go a long way to offset the heady sensation many people experience in foreign settings, where nobody knows them and nobody, they feel, cares what they do.

Well, except in areas that are mobbed by tourists, the traveler, as an outsider, possibly an "exotic," will indeed excite a lot of quiet interest among the locals.

One's status as a tourist is what offers the real protection, most of the time. Some countries allow a good deal more latitude in behavior to visitors than to citizens. As long as you conduct yourself reasonably and, again, discreetly, there should be no real problems.

But officer. . . . Sometimes, though, one does end up in tangles with the police. Remember that in many lands the cops are wretchedly paid and are presumed to supplement their incomes through shakedowns and similar tactics. Gays who are caught messing around are a prime target, of course.

Where this sort of thing prevails, if you plan to take any chances be sure to carry as little in cash and valuables with you as you can manage. And you might consider the cheap wristwatch ploy. Wear an inexpensive but flashy watch when you go prowling. Then, if you have to buy off an officer of the law, you can honestly say, and show, that you have very little cash with you, but that you will (reluctantly) consider giving up your precious wristwatch.

Do *not*, of course, try to bribe a cop in any country where this sort of salary enhancement is not the norm. The best way to find out what's expected is by consulting friends who've lived in the country. Guidebooks – even mainstream ones – occasionally provide information regarding the delicacy of police sensibilities, or lack thereof.

As a rough rule of thumb, efficiency signals honesty. The cop who wants you to pay off would rather not trouble you or himself with the jailing process. Indeed, the offense you have committed may be far less terrible than he had led you to believe. If he asks you to *walk* with him to the police station, the moment you two reach a quiet street, which is likely to be very soon, start wondering aloud if there may not be some simple way to settle this matter.

In addition to the police, there is the customs to consider. Everyone knows about not carrying drugs, but a good many other things are considered contraband, depending on the country. Recently it was reported that a man was arrested at the airport in Athens, Greece, for the crime of entering the country in possession of a "lewd object," i.e. a dildo. He got six months in jail. The lewd object had been a raffle prize, won by this unfortunate Greek gentleman in a gay bar during the course of a visit to an American city.

Not only sexual appliances but "inappropriate" clothing

could upset the man looking through your suitcase, and so might even gay guides. This is the case only in very uptight countries, and anyone visiting them would do well to copy the information from the guide and leave the volume at home.

U.S. Customs inspectors, remember, have a great deal of latitude, and while they can't actually arrest you unless they find something illegal, they can be a real pain if they see something they don't like. American Customs is considered one of the pissiest in the world.

Getting laid abroad. In many foreign countries there are few or no signs of any kind of organized gay life. "Gay" bars will be very mixed, and most of the men in them are likely to be wearing wedding rings. Gay life is there, of course, but connecting with it takes some patience. Generally, it's not hard to score if you keep your eyes open for subtle signals, are discreet about your gayness, and hang out where you can be approached by the types that attract you most. Despite the dampening news about AIDS, and whatever political messes are going at the moment, American gay men interest foreign gay men. And we do have a wide reputation for being wild, hot lays.

The gay traveler may have to expect to pay for sex, depending on where he visits. There are hustlers everywhere, but in some cultures presenting money or something of value dignifies relationships, in the local view, transforming them from casual, sordid encounters into something with a bit of class. In other cultures, where the only way of life is marriage, period, it's assumed that the man who seeks sex only with other males *should* pay for the privilege.

Still, if all seems hopeless, remember that in some countries every bellhop does some pimping, and many a waiter and beach boy is available.

Finally, English may not be the universal language, but it is widely known around the world. The man who approaches you because he would like to practice his English may or may not have something more interesting in mind.

Gay travel agencies

Travel arrangement for gays has become a specialty in recent years, and a gay travel agency can be a great help to the gay vacationer. With any kind of travel agent, though, it's best to make clear what you want and to ask questions about anything you have in mind regarding your trip. A friend of ours asked to be booked into a gay hotel on a journey to some far land. He had expected something free and easy, perhaps approaching an American steam bath in style, but found himself at a hostelry where the biggest excitement took place each afternoon in the parlor when tea was served.

Like most travel agents, the gay ones do a good deal of traveling, so they often have a lot of useful information. Be aware, though, that it may not be perfectly up to date.

Perils of togetherness

Lovers may live in the same apartment and it may seem to them that they spend all their hours in each other's company, but they probably work at different jobs in different locations and otherwise spend a certain amount of time away from each other, involved in their own groups of friends or in hobbies and interests the other half doesn't care for. In addition, their life is likely to be fairly set in a comfortable, secure daily routine.

When lovers travel together they are truly in each other's company incessantly, and they will be facing a certain number of novel stress situations. This combination can put heavy, possibly fatal, strains on even the closest relationship. But there are ways to minimize friction:

1. Don't go around the world on the first trip together. Start off with a relatively modest trip so you can get some idea how well you two might function on the grand tour.

2. Allow some breathing space. Go your separate ways now and again. Depending on the relationship and where you're traveling, this could mean wandering off in different directions for an afternoon, or it might mean taking separate overnight side trips.

3. Stay flexible. Neither should be forced to do something he really doesn't enjoy. If that means hitting the museums alone, well, so be it.

4. Be frank. The vibes between lovers may do well enough to keep life going smoothly at home, but while traveling it's

best to speak up. Suffering in silence only leads to trouble later.

5. Plan ahead, either jointly or with the responsibilities divided up. Arriving late at night in a strange city whose inhabitants speak some rare language very rapidly, and where you two have no room reservation, can set you to feeling edgy and to blaming each other for your plight.

Some couples and friends, sad to say, simply have no business traveling together. But separate vacations are fairly common among gay lovers. Nowadays there is a growing variety of vacation opportunities, including guided tours for gays, sea cruises, rafting, hiking, and theater holidays. Some men like highly organized situations, others want to be on their own. Since one guy's claustrophobia will be another's security blanket, lovers should discuss well beforehand just what their idea of travel is, and if they can't see eye to eye at all, they should consider going their separate ways. A vacation from each other often helps to recharge the relationship.

Nostalgia trips. Since many gays relocate far from their home town or city and spend years establishing a new life, we are especially open to the possibility of the nostalgia journey – going back to wherever after all these years. Often enough this desire is triggered by an invitation to a class reunion.

These can be fun as long as not too much is expected. Maybe your ex-classmates from good old Fillmore Consolidated High School have mellowed out, but the chances are excellent that the class clown is still telling strings of awful jokes, that the nerds of back then can't keep a conversation going even now, and that the corner-cutting finagler who knew all the angles has become the town's leading used car salesman.

Nostalgia trips can reawaken painful memories of growing up different, which may lead, particularly in reunion settings, to a desire to tell everyone off. In our experience, hardly anyone actually does this. Everyone is now older. Young Mr. Gorgeous, object of a secret crush once upon a time, may now be a very faded bloom, and the loathesomely arrogant football star could be fat and asthmatic and just out from under his latest bankruptcy. Maybe it's vivid with hurts and humiliations, but the past, one discovers, lives on only in the memory.

Finding information

Whether the gay man travels in the States or abroad, whether he goes mainly for culture or just for action, the more he knows in advance, the more time he'll have to enjoy his vacation. Some people enjoy "studying up" the place they plan to visit, reading and anticipating for some time beforehand. Others want the essentials in compact form and no more.

Every gay man should remember that however helpful the mainstream guidebooks may be, they will have little or no useful information about gay life. And, depending on the country visited, gay guides may be unavailable locally – may indeed, as we have pointed out, be banned. The best thing to do is to consult sources of gay information beforehand.

1. Gay guides. For the gay traveler within the United States and Canada two well-known books are useful, the *Gayellow Pages* and *Bob Damron's Address Book.* The former is updated from time to time and exists in a national and a number of regional editions. The latter is updated annually. Damron's guide concentrates on bars, restaurants, baths, and cruising spots. The other lists a wide variety of gay organizations and businesses, including bars and such, but no cruising places.

Of the international guides, the best known is *Spartacus,* widely sold in U.S. gay bookstores. It contains valuable discussions of the sex laws and customs of the various countries listed, along with helpful advice on fitting into the local gay scene and a listing of gay establishments. It's especially useful for the more out-of-the-way countries. The chief disadvantage is that it is too bulky to lug around, and for the man going into "iffy" lands, its cover and page illustrations could raise eyebrows at customs checks.

Private Stock International Directory (Christopher Street Book Shop, 500 Hudson Street, New York, New York 10014) is a compact pocket-sized guide with bar, bath, hotel, restaurant, and bookstore listings for a number of countries, including the U.S. and Canada, but little in the way of other information.

The international traveler should be aware that guides have

their limitations. The editors can't visit everywhere, so they depend on informants, who may or may not be reliable. An extreme example of this is an old, rather crudely printed guide to Europe, whose well-traveled author, it becomes obvious after reading a few pages, was interested only in rough trade. The book gives the impression that gay life is to be found only in slums and on waterfronts.

In another guide, one of Mexico City's dullest hotels, full of old straight couples and prim schoolteachers who tell their travel agent they must be in some place that's absolutely safe, is listed as a gay pickup scene. Well, maybe the listing made it so, livening up the usually three-fourths empty bar, but we assume some informant happened to luck out there once and simply assumed the spot was action central.

And of course gay places come and go. Since the information, correct or not, will be at least a year old by the time it gets into print, and possibly a good deal older, use the guides with wariness, and always get the newest one that's available.

2. *Newspapers and periodicals.* From time to time gay papers and magazines run travel pieces and feature articles about gay life in assorted foreign and domestic locales. This information is likely to be up to date and can be difficult to come by otherwise. Anybody who plans, even vaguely, a visit to some specific place would do well to file away any appropriate articles for future reference.

As soon as the traveler reaches his destination he should pick up the local gay paper or papers. Often they run directories of the local gay businesses and organizations.

3. *Literature.* Novels, short stories, travel essays and other non-fiction works about a country often give the traveler a better feel for the place than any guidebook. Don't scorn books written a number of years ago: a country's basic culture doesn't change very much, as a rule.

4. *Telephone directories.* Domestic guidebooks usually don't list telephone numbers. This can be inconvenient since gay restaurants and bars may be scattered throughout an unfamiliar city, and it is nice to know whether a place will be open

or even still in business before spending time and taxi fare. That's when the regular telephone directory comes in handy.

Generally, the telephone numbers of strictly gay establishments – as opposed to mixed ones – will be listed only in the white pages, if at all. Many all-gay spots have unlisted telephones.

If you do find a number, and you think the bar or whatever may no longer be gay, it's best not to ask point-blank, lest you get a uselessly vague answer. Instead, mention that you learned about the place in the such-and-such guide. If the establishment is gay, this "password" usually will get you all the information you need.

In your wanderings about a strange town you may spot a restaurant that looks like it might be gay, but isn't listed in your guidebook. To find out, look it up in the yellow pages of the phone book. A display ad in the classifieds means don't bother.

The charms and pleasures of travel are well known. But for the gay man to enjoy his visit to another part of his own country or another part of the world, it's best he do a little homework first, so his visit will go smoothly and, however wild it gets, safely.

THE NEW GAY WORLD AND YOU

12 Legally Gay

> ...it is not easy in a short time to do away with great prejudice.
>
> — Plato

That gay people might have legal rights is an idea that has only recently had widespread acceptance. Before World War II, gays in North America were officially criminals. In theory it was permissible to *be* homosexual as long as you didn't *do* anything. And this meant *anything* – merely congregating with other gays in public was unlawful, and any physical expression of gay sexuality could mean a term in prison.

Nowadays private consensual gay sex has been decriminalized in roughly half the states, and gay organizations can operate openly in most areas. So things have changed for the better. But we still have a long way to go. In many jurisdictions gay sex acts continue to be crimes, and in other ways we remain subject to frequent governmental discrimination. Gay establishments continue to be busted by the police, public display of affection between gays is still considered "lewdness" in most places, and our children can be taken from us, at the whim of authorities, for no reason other than that we are gay.

Nevertheless, as a group we are gradually emerging from being, when not on the wrong side of the law, in a legal limbo. The straight world – at least the responsible segment of it – now concedes that we exist in significant numbers, not as just a handful of aberrants. The notion is gradually taking hold that we constitute a minority whose members are entitled to society's benefits and protections.

Legislative action has brought about some improvement, but most of it has come out of successful challenges of restrictive regulations in courts of law. After World War II, groups seeking expansion of civil rights and curtailment of police abuses began to despair of persuading state and federal legislatures to take action. These organizations turned more and more to the courts, using as their primary argument the Bill of Rights.

At the same time the legal establishment was beginning to undergo a profound change, as it absorbed the thousands of new lawyers from diverse backgrounds, those who would never have been able to go to law school without the aid granted by the G.I. Bill.

And the country was changing: there was no longer near total refusal to recognize that whole groups of citizens were legally stigmatized by obvious injustices and denied the opportunity to participate in the society as equals.

The new legal liberalism was slow to deal with the problems of gays, until we began to come out in increasing numbers, starting in the sixties.

Today, despite improvements, the picture is not entirely a glowing one. Reform via the courts necessarily requires a piecemeal approach and has to be pursued through many separate tribunals, so progress usually is slow and success spotty. Generally speaking, over the years we've won more often than we've lost, but there have been setbacks. And recently certain groups, feeling the courts have gone too far in the area of civil liberties, have made concerted efforts to place more "conservative" – for which read "reactionary" – judges on the bench.

This should remind us that in one crucial respect the courts are little different from the legislatures. What has been done by the courts can be undone. All that's needed are a strong public outcry and the replacement of a rather small number of judges.

Liberal or conservative, the courts are likely to be the major arena for gay rights battles. Most legislatures don't want to touch these questions with a hundred-foot pole.

Aside from obviously crucial issues such as decriminalization and discrimination in employment and housing, certain areas of law promise to be important to gays for some years to come.

Parenting

Male or female, many gays become parents. In the past this usually occurred within a heterosexual marriage, but lately a number of alternatives have blossomed.

A gay parent in an intact heterosexual marriage usually has no legal problems to face. It's when a marriage begins to go awry that the trouble can start. The non-gay partner who discovers that he or she has been deceived about spouse's sexuality may conclude that the spouse is unworthy of trust, especially in regard to the children. Even when animosity is absent, it's a rare person who will not use a mate's gayness as a weapon should disagreements arise regarding child custody or visitation rights.

This means that even where the spouse knows the mate's true sexual orientation, the gay partner would be wiser not to discuss this with minor children, lest it be construed in court some day as an attempt to talk them into a "deviant lifestyle."

Formerly the courts almost universally deemed a gay parent automatically unfit to have custody of children, and visiting rights were often severely restricted. Judges have a good deal of discretion and how they exercise it is likely to be strongly influenced by local beliefs and opinions. A parent's homosexuality is still frequently considered a basis for denying child custody, especially in regions where conservative religious beliefs are dominant.

However, in recent years gay parents have been awarded custody of their children in a number of cases. Even when this happens, though, it's not unusual for the court to grant custody only on the parent's virtual celibacy, in order to set a "good example." Should a lover move in with the gay ex, the former spouse can go to court and get a custody or visitation order modified, so that the children may no longer even visit.

While dispassionate observers now agree that a parent's sexual orientation has little or no effect on the sexual preferences of his or her children, many courts, yielding to public pressure, are still inclined to curtail the contacts of gay parents with their children. Any gay person involved in child custody or visitation issues should have the assistance of an attorney, preferably one who is gay.

Second-hand parents. As any newspaper reader is aware, it's no longer particularly unusual for an unmarried woman to make a conscious decision to have a baby. And married couples who can't conceive offspring in the usual way are using a variety of new methods – test-tube fertilization, donor insemination, surrogate mothers – to accomplish this result. All this is giving the legal system fits, because the long-established principles of domestic relations are unable to deal with the new legal questions that have arisen.

This creates problems for gays. Over the years it has been fairly common for a lesbian who wants a child to have the sperm donated by a suitable gay male friend. If the sperm is passed via direct sexual intercourse, which probably is relatively rare, then the law has no problem in determining the legal father. But where some form of artificial insemination is used (the more likely approach in a lesbian–gay male arrangement), some novel legal questions are presented.

For instance, newspapers reported not long ago that the former lover of a lesbian mother sued for the right to be able to visit "her" child. It developed that the insemination had been accomplished using sperm from the ex-lover's brother, placed by her with a turkey baster where it would do the most good.

After a couple of flip-flops, the court finally approved an out-of-court agreement by which the ex would be allowed to see the child twice a month. There was no way the legal system could consider the ex to be the child's father. Visitation rights were granted because she was the child's aunt. And legally, because a turkey baster has no standing as a parent, the only possible conclusion the judge could reach was that the ex's brother was . . . Daddy.

Thus an act which may be intended as a favor for a friend can lead to a lot of problems. After all, any man who is legally identified as a child's father is obligated by law to support his offspring. Maybe the mother wouldn't dream of saddling this responsibility on a man who was only helping out, but circumstances can change. Mother could break with a lover and be left destitute. Mother could die. For some reason the state may have to take over support of the child. In that case, where the father can be identified, not even a written agreement with the mother will free him from responsibility.

Isn't it the same for straight married couples who resort to artificial insemination? Not really. Foremost, in our law there is an ancient doctrine: a child born to a couple who are legally married and living together is *conclusively* presumed to be the husband's natural child. The presumption has held firm in modern times, even where the husband has been shown by tests to be sterile. In the past many a noble lineage has thus been saved from the taint of bastardy, and at present, however illogical, it saves the courts a lot of trouble.

Also, artificial insemination of married women customarily is achieved via sperm from anonymous donors, with the agency that supplies the sperm sample guaranteeing to protect their identity.

Remember me? Child support is not the only hazard of second-hand parenting. Lately there has emerged a strong movement that supports the *right* of children to learn the identity of their biological parents. Started by people who were adopted, it has been taken up on behalf of offspring conceived by means of artificial insemination.

Proponents argue that their interest in their biological parents is more than mere curiosity. How else, they ask, can they know whether heredity predisposes them to certain medical conditions or genetic disease? How else can they find a blood relative who could serve as a donor for an organ transplant?

At least one legal jurisdiction has made a tentative decision which would require sperm banks to disclose the identity of donors, a ruling which upset just about everyone, but the ultimate outcome of this battle is far from decided.

Then there are the emotional hazards. As a young man the biological father may consider the whole thing a lark, just doing a favor for a friend. In later years, though, he may develop a certain amount of curiosity, even concern: is the child happy, well cared for? Is it getting the help in life which a father could provide?

From concern the biological father may wish to act. What are his legal rights? Can he get a court order permitting visitation? If he feels the child is being neglected or abused, can he get custody?

On the other side of the coin, a middle-aged gay man may be confronted by a son or daughter he's forgotten existed. Will the child be overjoyed at having found his long-lost father? Or will the child be angry and resentful?

What if a gay man's estate, left to his long-time lover, is claimed by the biological child of the deceased, product of a long-forgotten artificial insemination?

Lawsuits have been brought in all these areas, so far with varying results. Suits by offspring against their parents are not yet all that common, but they *do* occur. Under the laws of a number of states a man's child, forgotten though he or she might be, may very well have a valid claim on his estate. Much depends on how skilfully the will was drafted.

Sure answers will not be available until the law evolves to meet the problems posed by these types of parenting. But we are not likely to remain in a legal vacuum for long. That's because the heterosexual populace has interests that overlap ours, such as whether the identities of natural parents and sperm donors will be protected or not.

Gay couples

Some situations have not changed over the years. Gay marriage has remained a legal nullity. In the few states where the laws do not specify that spouses must be of opposite sexes, marriage licenses obtained by gay couples have turned out to give them no legal advantage.

The idea of "palimony" hasn't worked out well either. Most of the lawsuits filed to enforce "spousal" obligations between gay ex-lovers have been unsuccessful. Where financial recoveries have been made, the basis almost always has been the traditional legal principles concerning who owns what.

As many long-time gay couples are aware, wills and such can serve in place of legal marriage to define the partners' rights and obligations between each other. However, they have little effect on benefits provided from outside sources. Medical coverage, bereavement leave, and survivorship benefits, while commonly provided for families of married employees, are not available to persons in a gay relationship.

In several cities efforts have been made to alter this situation in regard to municipal employees. Reaction has been mixed. While insurance companies, interestingly, have not made any particular objection to this kind of proposal, they do have to know *whom* they are insuring. This means that the "partnership" must be recorded in some fashion. Here the problems begin. Moralistic sorts object strenuously, feeling that illicit relationships – gay or non-gay – should not be legitimized, made equivalent to marriage. Many proponents feel the partners should live together for a certain period before being eligible for benefits, perhaps six months as a minimum. They feel this eliminates the people who play musical bedrooms. But gays object to the requirement that the couple be sharing living quarters, pointing out that many same-sex couples find it convenient to have separate residences.

At this point it's impossible to predict what will happen with the "domestic partners" idea, but chances are very slight that it will ever be regarded by the courts as the legal equivalent of marriage.

Once it was fairly easy, in a number of states, for one lover to legally adopt the other. This not terribly common legal ploy has been meeting increased resistance in the courts of late. New York's highest tribunal has flatly rejected adoption "as a means of obtaining a legal status for a non-marital sexual relationship." In reaching its conclusion the court pointed out that parent-child sexual intimacy is repugnant in our society.

Safe at home?

Pull the door shut, slide the bolt, and you're home, free of the frustrations of the outside world. Everybody feels like that at times, whether home is a modest room or a chic penthouse. For gay men especially, the place called home has been of special importance. For many of us it's psychologically necessary to maintain our private space as a miniature and completely gay world, a counterbalance to the pervasively surrounding heterosexuality.

Until fairly recently in the history of gay life in the United States, home was the safest place for us to have our kind of sex and where we could enjoy such things as homoerotic books, sex toys, and skin flicks.

Its sanctity is assured by a number of court decisions. They covered a wide range of situations, but chiefly dealt with drug arrests and stolen property searches. Gay people have incidentally benefited from these rulings.

This may not seem terribly important nowadays. The "don't touch" rules in bars are relaxed in many areas, and sex can be had legally in baths and private clubs. Home is no longer the only place where male-male dancing can take place, or gay parties, or displays of affection between men.

However, the advent of AIDS has provided a pretext for renewing efforts to close down or severely restrict gay establishments. Depending on events, it's possible that the security of our homes from official intrusion may once again become vital to our survival as a sexual minority.

Ironically, though we benefit from earlier court rulings that have enlarged the rights of accused criminals, we may find ourselves taking it on the chin along with them if public pressure to "get tough" on crime has its way. Every legal decision that grants greater leeway to the police poses a potential danger to us. We would be wise to keep this in mind before we add our voices to those demanding that protections against unfettered police conduct be watered down.

How legal is gay porn?

Exactly *what* pornography is defies precise description, but it is *illegal* only if it is obscene. Thus, by the complicated legal definition presently in use, most material we call pornography in the United States is not obscene. So it is not against the law to own and enjoy it.

Well, there are some exceptions. There is a pale area in regard to heavy-duty S&M stuff. The major exception, though, is kiddie porn – so-called – which is anything that's sexually exploitive of children. There are even cases where sex education manuals intended for minors have become subject to prosecution.

There is a real danger that in the future, adult erotic materials could be banned on the basis that they *might* fall into the possession of children. This argument has been used in the past: it was basic to the anti-porno legal outlook in this country thirty years ago. Under this reasoning serious literature that deals openly with gay relationships can be suppressed.

If buying and possessing pornography is okay, selling or distributing it is another matter. A man who passes a hot magazine on to a friend or trades a VCR tape of *Blazing Jockstraps* for one of *Naked Surfers* has little to worry about, but anyone who goes into pornography as a business had better put some crackerjack lawyers on retainer first. Whether he manages to stay within the law or not, he is sure to be hassled.

The legal situation for gay people is far from perfect, and it varies from place to place. There is no guarantee that gains made will be preserved or augmented in the future. But consider that thirty years ago, in virtually any part of the United States or Canada, a gay man would be breaking the law by being in a gay bar, by cruising, by joining with other gays in a demonstration, by having gay friends over for a party, or by having sex in private. Enjoying such things as public dancing, pornography, or sex toys was out of the question.

We have come a long way in a relatively short period of time, legally speaking. We are wise to be aware of this and not take our rights for granted.

III
You and Gay Traditions

YOU AND GAY TRADITIONS

13 Sing Out, Louise

Now go out there and be so swell that you'll make me hate you!
—*Forty-Second Street*
(Warner Brothers, 1933)

To many of us, gay show business means only one thing, the drag record-show: in a bar in some I-hate-to-park-here neighborhood, out onto a tiny stage, one after another, totter men dressed as women, to mime the familiar lyrics of some song made famous by Marlene, Barbra, Edith, Judy, or Mae.

Well, the gay bar record-show is only a small part of gay show business, though no doubt that's where much of it began. But in most cities there are drag performances at a level significantly higher than the record act. Some bars feature occasional or regular shows with transvestites who actually can sing and dance.

At the professional level, a few drag troupes tour the country, with the Jewel Box Revue being the oldest and best known. In relatively recent years a number of high-camp groups have come into being, like the Hysterical Theater Company, with such attractions as *Camille* starring Charles Ludlam, and the Ballets Trockadero de Monte Carlo. New York City is favored with another ballet troupe, The Gloxinia, and an all-male opera company, La Grand Scena.

The Cockettes and other genderfuck groups, who make no attempt to hide masculine characteristics while wearing female attire, have for the most part gone the way of bell-bottoms and love beads, but the Angels of Light puts on an occasional production in San Francisco.

Then there are individual drag stars, the most famous today being Jim Bailey and Charles Pierce. Bailey specializes in almost spookily perfect re-creations of famous singers. Pierce gives us immortal movie actresses, and he's probably responsible for more *bons mots* than anyone since Oscar Wilde.

Curiously, some drag shows are deliberately aimed at straight audiences. The show at Finocchio's in San Francisco has been running for over forty years, but it would die overnight were it not for the tour buses pulling up at the door. The "tourist show" means the entertainers must take time to win over the audience – which has come to see "freaks" – and must straighten out and dull down their jokes. As a rough rule of thumb, the gayer the audience, the more fun the drag entertainment.

Sweet charity. A wide range of gay organizations put on benefits and fundraisers. In the main, they take the form of variety shows or revues. Many are produced at a near-professional level, but from act to act the quality may vary from first-rate to godawful. And some of these annual extravaganzas are not the kind of thing you'd want to take Great Aunt Agatha to see. Bike and buddy club productions often revel in raunchy humor and should be checked out by anybody who enjoys butch bawdiness.

Sons of Thespis. Gay theater companies, found in our larger cities as a rule, are of two kinds. There's the Serious Theater Group, where the acting is uneven but sincere as hell, the sets show what miracles can be wrought by a clever guy with some corrugated paper and a staple gun, and the auditorium smells faintly of whatever it was previously used for. These companies are always functioning on ridiculous budgets, but they do manage to present new and often worthwhile plays about gay life. No one else is doing this, and mighty few acting groups of any kind offer plays by nobodies, which in the theater world is more daring than going over Niagara Falls in the proverbial barrel.

Then there's a more commercial brand of gay theater. Here

the principal dramatic impulse is to place on the stage for extended periods of time one or more basically nude young men. The play's title is always a tip-off, being something like *My Hustler Lost His Drawers.* True, a perfectly legit play might require a young man with a gorgeous body and impressive qualifications to lounge about undressed – we can think of several dramatic works that do and a number of others that would benefit immensely from just that. But there's a discernible difference in motivation.

The future of the meat show on such a pretentious level probably is dim. Via the various media nowadays, we are amply and inexpensively supplied elsewhere with naked bodies, lousy plots, corny dialogue, and the feeling of having wasted our time.

Some adult movie theaters of the gay persuasion provide live entertainment that is usually a good deal more frank, and at least as straightforward about its intentions. After the hunky young man dances out onto the stage to the rhythms of taped rock, he surmounts the eternal problem of getting out of a pair of tight jeans gracefully, and what comes next varies with local ordinances but can get very intimate indeed. From the observer's point of view the act can be exciting in a divinely trashy way, or it can be – if one notices needle tracks on one arm, say – rather depressing.

Closet drama. Recently we went with some hetero friends to a long-running Broadway production. They came away wondering what the hell it was all about. To them the frenzied actions of the characters had little discernible motivation. We, however, having picked up a clue left here and there by the playwright, had no problem. One of us said to our friends, "Suppose the two roommates, instead of being two macho-stud skirtchasers, are gay, and suppose Miss Easylay is a male, then . . . you see?" They did and were astounded, and they decided they felt a bit used by the author of the play. So did we.

As in the novel, the process of turning Albert into Albertine has been going on for a long time in the theater. It's obvious in many of Noel Coward's works, in some of the plays by Tennessee Williams, and, alas, in productions by living playwrights. Perhaps the day will come when gay writers will no longer feel it necessary to engage in this sort of subterfuge. In the meantime, there's a lot more gay theater going on than may be apparent to the straight or the naive.

Gay show business and you

It should be clear that a fair amount of gay entertainment, ranging from humble to grand, goes on in large and many fair-sized cities. Evidence of this activity is not widely broadcast, though, so a man with an interest in gay show business should watch the ads in gay papers and check the posters and flyers in gay businesses and bars.

One's interest in entertainment can easily extend beyond observing. Yes, it's usual to think of show biz as accessible only by hardhearted clawing, good connections, and casting oneself incessantly upon the couch. In much of gay show business, however, a man with useful abilities is likely to be welcomed. Becoming involved with local gay entertainment activities is a good way to get one's toes wet in show biz, develop an enjoyable leisure time activity, or maybe even begin a professional career.

You say you're interested, but you feel you have no special talent, and you don't own even one dress. Remember that there's a backstage, too. No need to sit there alone in your room when you can become an impresario. That is, why not stage a bar show? A nice little variety show to run two or three times on a weekend night, that sort of thing.

Oh, of course you can. Just follow these guidelines and take these handy hints, starting off with this useful generality: the most willing and helpful performers will be drag artistes. It's easier, then, to present an all-drag show, but mixed productions get a wider audience.

Once you have found an agreeable bar owner, the next step is to get a stage constructed, just a simple platform in the back of the room. On the wall behind it hang a curtain made of strips of tinsel. Nothing else will do, not lamé, not Aubusson tapestry.

1. Sound. The sound system is inevitably a problem, so don't let it worry you. It's usual to pipe the sound through the jukebox speakers. The result will be loud, but it'll have a lot of bass, an esthetic shortcoming sanctified by years of tradition. If you can arrange something better, at not too much effort and expense, do it: the difference in quality will delight performers and audience both.

Carefully check the microphone. It should not amplify even the lightest human touch, it should not produce squeals from time to time, and it should not give electric shocks to anyone who touches it.

Decide where to station the sound man. Remember that it helps in cueing music if he can see the stage. The guy you pick for this assignment should have, besides technical knowledge, a calm, sober, unflappable nature, steadiness in crises, tolerance of human foibles, and a burly physique.

You see, his problems begin when the various entertainers bring in cassette tapes of the music they want played for their acts. Many show biz personalities, famous or obscure, believe "all that technical stuff" is taken care of by "somebody." This means their inept home recording job should sound perfect when the sound man plays it. And it means that they expect cassettes to cue themselves. Inevitably, performers' tapes have more than one number on them, on the chance that all those wonderful people out there in the dark will want an encore. Occasionally some unscrupulous type will "miscue" his tape, setting it to the song just before the scheduled one. He'll look surprised when it comes on, then shrug, and in the time-honored way he'll go on with the show. Having thus expanded his act, he can blame the sound man for the "accident."

In fact, everyone will blame the sound man for all kinds of things he hasn't any control over. It's not fair, but it's inevitable. Pick yours well.

2. Lights. There *must* be a follow spot, even if it has to be rented. The operator should be as thin as possible, have a good body and a cute ass. That's because the follow spot very likely will have to be placed where it interferes with the view of a goodly number of the audience, so you should be sure these folks have *something* to look at.

Compared to the sound system, running the light is easy. It's to be kept on the performer at all times.

*

3. Backstage. Just as most bars don't have permanent stages, neither do they have dressing rooms. Frequently one of the restrooms is pressed into use, though, with luck, a more spacious area may be available, like a hallway, a storage room, or the manager's office. If there's no room indoors, consider the alley in back. Assuming good weather and tolerant neighbors, a dressing area of parked cars and vans or possibly a tent can be set up. Don't worry too much about this: entertainers will bear with a great deal for the pleasure of appearing before a live audience.

4. Up front. A minor problem may arise with any performers who have their own personal breasts. Much as a man with a new car likes to "just drive it around the neighborhood," the proud possessor of a Real Pair may want to put them on display. After all, whether by hormones or surgery, they are expensive, and they may not last forever; silicone often hardens into something resembling a baseball. The law, fortunately, tends to lag behind daily reality, so any moldy local ordinance against baring the bosom is sure to apply only to cupcakes of the genetically feminine variety.

5. Stars, stars, stars. Now for the cast. Essentially you may have to take what you can get, but try for balance and variety. Let's start with the drag performers. Some imitate famous ladies and some don't, but essentially there are four basic types: the beauty, the waif, the frump or comic, and the broad. Avoid having too many in any one category. And don't use a TV who has little definition. What she's like in real life isn't important, but if she hasn't a good strong personality when in drag, she will be no more entertaining than are most men in dresses.

Record acts can be good but usually aren't. Try to get transvestites who can sing or dance.

Otherwise, it shouldn't be too hard to find different kinds of acts for the show. Some gay men have little "living room routines" they do, and one or two of these can add a nice humorous touch to the proceedings.

Your show can be livened by using bodybuilders for decorative effect here and there. Some of them may have posing routines that make a nice act.

6. *Leadership time.* Then comes the great test of your skills as a diplomat, setting up the order of the show. Everybody will want to be on last. Obviously that's impossible, but *do not discuss this matter with the entertainers.* Just figure out the best arrangement you can make. You task will be a little easier if you are scrupulously fair in matters of time and if there are to be several performances or a brief run of the show. In that case you can vary the order of the acts.

However you decide matters, type up the list, date and sign it so it looks official, and pin it on the wall in the dressing room. You may still have a few shouting matches, but don't believe anybody who threatens to quit the show. Hang tough, and above all, don't argue: that way lies doom.

Okay, so these are friends, bar buddies, maybe customers, and you don't like all this friction. But everybody knows the buck has to stop somewhere, so your firmness will be appreciated more than you may realize.

7. *Perils.* Whatever the "backstage" area is, the participants will have a drink or two before the show. Occasionally a performer will drink a great deal too much, "for my nerves. Opening nights are just hell." What to do? You can forbid the artiste to go on, but probably you won't be taken seriously. Your only choice may be to lock this person in a handy closet or basement with a bottle of booze. Protests will be loud at first, but after a while they will die away. Perhaps this sounds like an extreme action. But it isn't when you consider that, short of total restraint, the drunk performer *will* go on.

The safety of the audience is important. If a danseuse topples onto a customer, for instance, injury and lawsuit may bloom. It's true that in most bar shows a certain informality and camaraderie reign, especially at the second show of the night, so people seated in the first row won't mind their laps sat upon, their lovers flirted with, or feathers floating down into their drinks. But make it clear to the performers that there are limits: they should stay well away from the edge of the stage when being wildly active, customers' toupees should not be lifted, and bald men should not have the tops of their heads kissed more than once a show.

For reasons we discuss later on, the bar show, being a gay

social function, always starts late. But do try to keep this under control. The tardier the performance, the rowdier the audience and the more nerve-wracked the artistes.

If the show runs appreciably longer than an hour, for the sake of beverage sales and healthy bladders, do schedule an intermission.

Just before and all during the performance, stay backstage. Partly, you will be needed because there is concentrated the essence of the heartbreak and triumph of show business for the participants: perfectly rational beings may become difficult under pressure or in drag or both. And they lose things. You must be a major calming force. Neglect this, and disaster will follow. For instance, at a recent show we saw, Miss Leather Lady came out to do her act. It became clear that she had forgotten her all-important bullwhip when this item was so graciously brought out to her by the next performer in the program. This was the exotic Estrelita, who entered dressed in a gown that looked like it had been made by Acme Fireworks Company, then took her time delivering the vital prop and making her exit. Leather Lady finished her number and, whip in hand, hurried backstage. That was one show that did not go on.

8. *Good evening, folks.* It's a good idea to have an MC open the show and introduce the acts. You might want to do this job yourself. Remember, if you introduce one of your performers as "the faaaa-bulous," introduce all of them that way.

There are a couple of things to note about drag entertainers. Anyone wearing a dress, however grotesquely unsuitable for such garb and of whatever sex, is *she.* Also, it's customary for appreciative members of the audience to approach transvestite performers while they are on the stage and place a dollar bill in the lowest plunge of the gown's neckline. This sort of activity may be inconvenient, but don't discourage it. Genuine or prearranged, it can go far to make the drag's evening. And in charity functions the money collected in this manner is often donated to the worthy cause.

9. *Finale.* At the end of the show it's proper and usual to thank everybody who helped with it, including the light man, for

"the great job" he did, and the sound man, "who's done just an amazing job considering all the problems he's had to deal with tonight." Then, if the show is a fundraiser, it's customary to announce the "take." Just give the gross. It might be too depressing to subtract overhead costs just now.

With thanks to the audience and a goodnight, the MC ends the proceedings, and your work as a gay show business impresario is done, except that you should buy the light man, the sound man, and yourself a round of drinks. Order doubles.

YOU AND GAY TRADITIONS

14 Withering Camp?

Merle Oberon (as George Sand) to Cornel Wilde (as Frederic Chopin): "You could write miracles of music in Majorca."

— *A Song to Remember*
(Columbia, 1945)

The camp mode of viewing life has flourished quietly among gay men for a long, long time. In recent years, however, camp has become the focus of a good deal of attention, not all of it favorable.

Among younger gay activists camp is seen as a leftover from the Bad Old Days of oppression and scorned as something snobbishly elitist and separatist, politically unengaged, and loaded to the brim with gay self-hatred. They hope that camp will die out, but other people feel that, far from being on its deathbed, the camp sensibility is becoming more widespread, moving out into the non-gay world.

We feel these views are both off the mark, because they fail to consider what camp really is and what needs is has served among gay men.

Let's get the hard part over with first and try to determine what camp is. ". . . I admit it's terribly hard to define," a gay man says to a straight friend in Christopher Isherwood's novel, *The World in the Evening.* "You have to meditate on it and feel it intuitively." Susan Sontag in her well-known essay, "Notes on Camp," calls it a sensibility, which, as ". . . distinct from an idea . . . is one of the hardest things to talk about."

Right on both counts. But in addition to the problem posed in defining a sensibility, camp is difficult to pin down because every man is the captain of his own taste. This makes camp a hugely subjective matter, largely free of objective standards. It's almost all grey areas. As Esther Newton puts it, in *Mother Camp: Female Impersonators in America,* "Camp inheres not in the person or thing itself but in the tension between that person and the context of the association."

Fortunately for the existence of this chapter, though, some persons and things are almost always perceived as camp by anyone with the camp sensibility. Other people and objects are nearly always seen as outside that definition. So camp does have *some* identifying characteristics.

Emotionally camp most often is humorous. Sometimes the humor is overt, but more often it's low-keyed, subtle.

Criticism and judgment are almost absent. A person or thing is camp or it isn't. This means that there is no such thing as bad camp. Even a bad try at creating camp might very well create it, especially if not in the way the creator intended.

Content is not the focus of the camp sensibility. Style is. This is probably the reason so many straights and even some gays have trouble understanding what camp is. Anything with physical form has willy-nilly some sort of style. This means the camp way of seeing life opens up great vistas of appreciation, including areas which, in terms of giving artistic gratification, are generally considered worthless desert.

But there are limits: the camp sensibility feeds on artifice, on human ways of being, on man's creations, but rarely or never on nature. Yosemite and Grand Canyon, for instance, are too real to be anything but themselves. On the other hand, in some few works of high art and other great creations of the human mind where content and style merge extremely well, the result is much too transcendent, too powerful to be camp. Beethoven's late quartets, as an example, could hardly be called campy.

Art, junk, kitsch, camp. This isn't to say that good art can never be camp, that only junk will serve. Some things and people are capable of affecting us on more than one level. A Tiffany lamp (and we're talking the real thing here, not imitations), is generally considered a camp object. But it's also a carefully wrought creation, a work of art. The opera *Aïda* is a masterpiece and also an outstanding example of camp. Bette Davis of the stylized gestures and clipped speech is camp, but she's also a fine actress who has given a number of brilliant performances.

While it's true that junk does provide a lot that stimulates the camp perception, this area gets very tricky. Much failed or half-assed art can be camp, but a great deal just doesn't make it. This stuff is called *kitsch*.

Speaking broadly, kitsch is anything created by artistic means for non-artistic ends. It doesn't exist for its own sake, and it can't be called a failure. Within its own usually very low level of aspiration, a kitsch piece is almost always quite successful. As an example of kitsch, take a little ceramic puppydog with a sweet smile on its face. Here artistic means are used to evoke a certain reaction from the susceptible observer: "Oh, how cuuuuute!"

The doggie *could* be turned into a camp object merely by placing a miniature noose around its neck and hanging it somewhere, perhaps as a decoration on the wall. Instant low camp.

Where junk *is* camp is where artistic failure literally creates a highly individual style. Should the kitschy puppydog be made not out of clay, glaze, and paint, but out of ivory and sapphires, then it would be a camp object, because of the immense contrast between content and its means of expression, its style. Like this, anything that displays a malproportion between content and expression is very likely to be noticed and appreciated by the camp-tuned observer, who may well find this to be more intriguing than mere artistic perfection. Something that's 'off' can be appreciated for both what it aims to be and fails at being, and at the same time. That's why bad art and other more or less ungainly human creations have so much to offer the camp sensibility.

Camp humanity. We have concentrated on *things*, so far, but people also can be camp objects. For obvious reasons this is especially true where individuals are presented as bigger than life – in the theater, movies, television. Again, it's emphatic style that makes for camp. A classic example of the wholly created persona would be the late Mae West. And, as with objects, quality doesn't matter. Anyone who is charming at being bad, or bad at being charming, may create a total effect that adds up to a strongly defined personality that can appeal as camp. But this doesn't happen every time.

Maria Montez made a series of Arabian Nights and South Seas movies with Jon Hall, Sabu, and Turhan Bey. So did her successor at the same studio, Yvonne de Carlo. Yvonne's films have their moments, but to anyone with the camp mentality, Maria's are far more fascinating. Perhaps the reason is, oddly enough, that Maria took her roles seriously but Yvonne let a little bit of camp get into her interpretations.

Many of the media stars who are considered camp project a certain amount of androgeny as part of their being. Joan Crawford, "our lady of the shoulders," hardly came across as the most femme of leading ladies in her films. Interest in combining aspects of both sexes into one being is also expressed in a preoccupation with role reversal, as in transvestism. Almost all drag is camp, whether intended or not. Form and content have small chance of meeting in unity. Only where the transvestite succeeds completely in creating the illusion of the opposite sex can there be no camp.

Camp and the calendar. The camp sensibility is time-haunted. Often enough the passage of time gives style to objects and persons, especially as preserved in some form of aural or visual recording, and usually very much at the expense of content. Back in 1910 a postcard showing a nude woman would likely have caused most of its viewers to flash lustfully on its content. Today the same plump Gibson girl with sugary smile and stacks of hair would impress far more as camp than as erotica.

Time, as the ultimate quality test, destroys many things as works of art, turning them into camp objects. Take Gounod's opera, *Faust.* Please. It was highly regarded by critics and for many years extremely popular with the public. Today its richly sacred tone strikes us as only religiosity, its music as mere crowd-pleasing twaddle, and its libretto as a silly boy-meets-girl concoction. In the present day it's difficult to think of *Faust* as anything *but* camp.

Although the main feeling in camp is humor, time's artifacts may bring with them a different, minor-key emotion. Something or someone once chic, now passé, once admired, now forgotten, can be rather forlornly touching. Thus in some camp we find a certain amount of pathos. After a solid run of several centuries in art and literature, pathos has become rather old-fashioned in this day and age – a camp emotion, perhaps?

Roots of camp

Now that we have some idea of what camp is, in order to find out where it is headed we should examine where it comes from – what makes it what it is and why it exists at all.

"Camp is not a thing," Esther Newton writes. "Most broadly it signifies *a relationship between* things, people, and activities or qualities, and homosexuality."

Yes, and starting very early on: typically the gay child, aware of his sexual orientation or not, perceives himself as somehow different from his peers. This may exist as an inner feeling, or it may be engendered by external events such as being made fun of or being rejected by his playmates. The gay child usually experiences this sense of difference as negative, and as a rule he has two ways to deal with it.

One is play-acting. The child who is overtly no different from his peers wants to stay that way. Even if he hardly knows what he is doing he will make an effort to go along with the crowd, fake an interest in much that he doesn't find all that interesting. After all, he is not only keeping his friends, but also getting praise from his parents for socializing so nicely.

The other way is to withdraw from a painful, rejecting world. The child who follows this option will come to depend more on his imagination than upon other people for amusement and company, and will seek out stimulation for his musings in the readily available popular arts: TV, movies, comic books, pop music and such. Though he may be criticized by adults for being a loner and for not enjoying endless hours of athletic competition, often he may also find a certain amount of support within the family. Some parents like their offspring to show signs of culture. "He reads almost too much, I sometimes think," Mom says proudly to the neighbors. And the Oedipal drama may offer reinforcement: "I just can never get my husband to go to the movies, so it's been delightful since Bobby's become so interested. He and I go all the time now. I call him my date."

All children, it's true, use withdrawal and pretense to deal with their problems, but gay children may use them a great deal more than others.

Big boy now. As an adult the gay man's feeling of being different usually gets a big boost when he realizes he is a member of a not always warmly greeted minority. Almost inevitably he is going to feel rather detached from the world, perhaps even becoming bitterly or resignedly alienated.

The great fuss made about hetero sex – all those bikinied, stacked young females ten times life size on billboards, all those gorgeous men lusting after gorgeous women in media entertainments – can only reinforce the gay man's perception that life is structured to serve an outlook that he does not share.

The grownup gay man's interest in the arts, perhaps developed during a troubled adolescence, easily may continue, bringing him not only pleasure, occupation, and refuge, but also the company of other gay men with interests and outlooks similar to his. He may have a good deal of time and money to spend on enjoying the arts, high or low, since he is likely to have few family cares and little or no involvement with the concerns of the straight world.

This is nice, but as the saying goes, all roses have thorns: what a gay man likes the most, especially if it lies in an area of the arts that's advanced, costly, antique, or esoteric, may not always be readily available for enjoyment. What is most easily at hand he may not find particularly rewarding. Since the arrival of the industrial age most of the world's goods have been made to please the greatest number. This includes not only furniture and clothing and such, but also much in the popular and public arts. So much here is so obviously and repetitiously derivative from better models, and so plainly simple-minded, that the stuff is difficult to even pay attention to, much less enjoy for what it is.

In short, as Susan Sontag puts it in "Notes on Camp," "The

relation between boredom and Camp taste cannot be overestimated." That is, there is *no way* to perceive many of our most prominent amusements and diversions as they are intended to be perceived.

The choice lies between rejection and acceptance. Total rejection calls for an ivory tower stance that is extremely difficult to manage for most people because it is so very expensive. Not everyone can build himself a Hearst Castle and stock it with antiques and the perfect blonde. Acceptance is possible only on another level, one that is non-heterosexually valued, detached, and personal.

Many a gay man, having become adept at play-acting early in life, will continue it in adult life. Everybody does some public pretending, but for gays, putting on a good show has been extremely important. Depending on circumstances, it can mean the difference between a career or a succession of unrewarding jobs, being a member of a cherished family group or an outcast, and even remaining alive or getting killed.

Certainly the more closeted the gay man, the more complete his impersonation, but even the liberated gay man faces situations where he feels it's best to switch on his acting abilities. One man will play-act only at work, another only when putting the make on a straight man, a third never except when visiting dear, kind Grandma, who is too ill, old, and mind-locked to deal with any shocking revelations. And late at night on a shadowy street nobody who's sane, seeing a group of loutish teenagers coming the other way, is going to greet them with, "Hi, guys. I'm gay."

Anyone who is going to act a part, even for a short time, must be able to pick up cues, so many a gay man will develop a heightened sensitivity to what's going on in his vicinity.

All this adds up to produce, often enough, an adult gay man with a highly tuned sense of awareness of what's emotionally authentic in both life and art, and what's false. Since the world of surface appearances is the prettiest one of them all, this ability may not be the most comfortable one to have, but it is basic to the camp sensibility.

So nature and circumstance put the gay man in a position to see the world from the unique angle of the observer of a world that is not his. Though aware of the generally held standards, he isn't required to take them all that seriously, because he isn't profiting much by them himself, having to hide his true nature or be rejected. Therefore, what is to stop him from seeing content as style? Why not look for humor where others only find the utmost seriousness? And if, as a consequence, the seriousness of every thing and person deemed camp is lessened or banished, so what?

After all, the camp sensibility exists to give amusement, so in its quiet, harmless way camp is rather sweepingly subversive. And not only because it plays games with human values, but also because it has been made to serve the purpose of giving gay men a sense of belonging, of self-worth, of living in a world of their own.

The anti-camp camp. Historically, camp's source is in the preliberation conditions under which gay men have long lived. So it's no wonder that the more activist sorts among us, particularly the younger ones, look askance at camp. And they are right when they say it is elitist, separatist, and politically passive.

The sense of self-worth that camp can give degenerates rather easily into mere snobbery and the old but baseless notion that gay men are, by nature, more "artistic" than other humans on this planet. Camp is separatist in that it defines *us* from *them* pretty thoroughly. It's passive, a way of watching the world pass by. Politics and politicians, seen from the camp perspective, are low camp at best and probably mere kitsch.

We can't agree, however, with those who feel that camp is a bearer of gay self-hatred. In its passivity camp simply reflects the limited options gay men have had. As a means of finding amusement, camp is a clever set of maneuvers, but rather desperate as well, getting blood from a stone. That self-worth had to be sought from this ghetto sensibility suggests how difficult it was to come by any other way.

However, what many people don't see about camp is its uncritical and wholehearted acceptance of people and things. Camp admires or ignores, nothing more. Admiration is a kind of affection. If anything, camp is a reaction to self-hatred. It gives those who are tuned to it a way of loving much, if not all, of the sometimes ugly and often difficult world we live in.

Straight camp? In discussing where camp is going, the first thing to say is that it is extremely unlikely to be going straight. A few heterosexuals, particularly actors, *may* have developed a true camp sensibility, but most of them haven't the motivation. Anybody who thinks differently should complete both these exercises:

1. List some examples of camp consciously created by somebody straight. (Warning: Cecil B. De Mille movies don't count. Believe it or not, he had no intention of creating camp; he *thought* he was making works of art. Bette Midler doesn't count; she's the exception that proves the rule.)
2. Assist a straight person in understanding camp.

This brings us to Susan Sontag, who makes an admirable effort to analyze camp in her pioneering essay, "Notes on Camp," where she writes, "While it's not true that Camp taste *is* homosexual taste, there is no doubt a peculiar affinity and overlap." But Sontag misses the point in concluding that camp taste stems from the dandyism of past centuries, "an aristocratic posture with relation to culture" indulged in by "small urban cliques." This suggests that camp taste can only develop under conditions of leisure, education, and massive doses of culture. Certainly these advantages wouldn't hurt any, but in our experience a great many gay men with backgrounds that are nothing so moneyed and taste-laden have a highly developed camp sensibility. In our acquaintance the person with the greatest sense of camp, who sees all the world through camp-colored glasses, is a small-town junior high school dropout speedhead transvestite who makes change in a porno film arcade.

Fascinating as her essay is, it's possible that Sontag generalized too strongly from experience with only one small urban clique. But the best-intentioned heterosexual observer is likely to be misled, since in our experience most gay men share their sense of camp only with one another.

Whither camp?

Within the gay world camp's days may be numbered. It is reasonable to expect that a ghetto mentality eventually will fade away when the conditions that created it weaken and disappear. But for now, while it's true that immense progress has been made in recent years, the childhood experiences of gay men have changed little if at all, and many adult gays still live under conditions that are essentially those of the Bad Old Days. A number of gay men still remain more or less closeted. So, we suspect that the gay sensibility, if not immortal, will be with us for some time to come.

Some may see this as counterproductive for future gains in gay life. However, being passive, camp basically is a recreational way of seeing, and not useful for actively dealing with daily life problems. Few gay men can or want to operate completely within the camp sensibility. So it's quite possible to march or picket in the afternoon and enjoy a showing of *Storm Over Lisbon* in the evening. After all, what is camp but something to enjoy for the pleasure it gives? As a portable, sophisticated, adult form of play, camp may live on well beyond its usefulness. We can't see anything wrong with that.

YOU AND GAY TRADITIONS

15 Some Native Folkways

> If our fledgling culture fails us, it will be because we forgot how to question it, forgot how to laugh at it....
>
> — Armistead Maupin

Here we'd like to consider some of the ways we are. Let's begin with a household item that has excited the gay sensibility for hundreds of years.

I. Chandeliers

The true importance of this illumination device became clear to us only recently, on the night we went to a party in what turned out to be a top candidate for the world's gayest apartment. How gay was it? Well, the living room floor covering looked like pink angora, and we shuddered to think how many harmless acrylics had been hunted down and killed to create it. Between the living room and the dinette a narrow passageway was almost blocked by two étageres that faced each other, all brass and glass. We edged past into the small dining room and found a friend. He was standing at the far side of the heavily canapéd table, filling his plate. When we greeted him and he looked up and smiled, it was then that we realized we were looking at one another literally through a huge chandelier. Its lowest lustres dangled hardly two feet above the surface of the table, a problem created by the fact that our host's condo contempo apartment had nine-foot ceilings.

Looking at this oversized beauty, it was hard to imagine that the chandelier began as very butch and ugly, back in the Middle Ages, when it was nothing more than a ring of crudely hand-wrought metal with spikes on which to impale fat, dirty-gray candles.

Then came the Renaissance in Europe. More tiers were added, and elaborations began to appear. Then the chandelier was taken up in a big way by the French court. Kings Louis XIII (gay), XIV, XV, and XVI (straight but heavily into decor), found life at Versailles unbearable without quantities of chandeliers. They liked them made with lots of that new and expensive "in" material, imported from Venice or Bohemia, called glass. While the populace footed the bill, the chandelier as we know it evolved, with the ropes of sparkling, faceted beads, masses of pendant lustres, and huge central blobs of rock crystal.

Historical note: The earliest surviving chandelier in the United States hangs in the Old North Church in Boston. As befits that shrine of patriotism, it is quite simple, made of brass and having a mere two tiers. An English import, it was hung in 1725.

Back in Europe chandeliers continued to grow and grow until finally, about the middle of the last century, they came to be constructed to monstrous size. This was in accordance with high Victorian taste, which also dictated that their design be eclectic. That is, one could proudly possess a Gothic–Louis-XV–Egyptian number, assuming one had the ceiling for it and the stomach as well.

Such excess and new technologies combined to bring about the fall of the chandelier. First came kerosene illumination, then gas lighting, and finally electricity. The pitiful wax candle was doomed. A few incandescent bulbs easily provided as much light as a great mass of tapers.

In the spirit of progress, many chandeliers were wired for Mr. Edison's new invention. But the bulbs shone too brightly. To bring the ghastly glare back to the warm glow, lots of little lampshades were added. Even the Victorians had to admit this looked damned silly.

Then came Art Nouveau, and it was all over for the chandelier. The newfangled desk and floor lamps, made in the form of exotic plants or angry cobras, were sometimes rather creepy looking, but they triumphantly demonstrated the advantages of reflected and indirect lighting.

The chandelier, by all expectations, should have ended up in museums, attics, and dumps. However, grossly outmoded, they still tinkle all over the place. What could explain this rare instance of survival of the unfittest? Well, chandeliers are useless only on the boring, practical, everyday level of life. That's like the basement of a house, where people go, though perhaps frequently, only when they have to. On the higher planes of existence the chandelier adds glamour and romance, a sense of the past, a feel for the grand style, a fondness for history as told by MGM in Technicolor with Linda Darnell.

No wonder gay men have a special feeling for this kind of lighting fixture. Whose heart beats faster at the sight of a tensor light or a sixty-watt bulb? Whose complexion is flattered by the rays of a fluorescent tube? With his dinette stuffed full of chandelier, our host may not exhibit a perfect sense of proportion in decor, but no doubt the reasons for what he has done are beautiful.

II. Gentrifying

In formerly decaying neighborhoods such as Chelsea in New York, the South End in Boston, Montrose in Houston, Oak Lawn in Dallas, Lincoln Park in Chicago, the Marquette University area in Milwaukee, the Summit–Grand Avenue area in St. Paul, Capitol Hill in Denver, Hillcrest in San Diego, and the Western Addition and Alamo Square in San Francisco, gay men have been a major force in reclaiming, house by house, entire residential blocks, restoring them to splendor here and there, or at least to respectability. We are now society's premier gentrifiers. In many cities it's become unfashionable in some gay circles to live in a late twentieth-century building.

Gentrifying makes sense for gay men. Few of us have any reason to be directly concerned about the quality of inner city public schools. We're willing to move into a still-tough area. And we are oriented toward life in or about the central city, since that's where many of us work and most of us play.

In town after town there are once-good to absolutely-grand

neighborhoods, where one residence after another is a treasure hidden underneath the grime of the years, the neglect of poor upkeep, and misguided attempts at modernizing and remodeling. With carved marble fireplaces, high ceilings with sculpted rosettes, parquet floors and ornamental cornices, obviously that's the sort of place that has *style.* Who could resist?

Fortunately, most cities have no shortage of these gems. And even where there are few or none available, as in Los Angeles, gentrifiers are still busy at work. There they buy modest tract houses, often of the Roaring Twenties Mission style, and face them with French townhouse mansards, two-story doors copied from Beverly Hills mansions, and surgically shaped shrubbery. Or they make the house into a neoclassical Wedgwood temple, complete with pillars and a large statue filling the front porch.

Yes, the gentrifying urge is a strong one, and for those who have it, there is nothing like finding a house with promise, and no thrill like ripping out a modern partition to find behind it an oak-paneled wall in perfect condition.

And everywhere the gentrifiers gather, real estate agents are happily rubbing their hands as they point out to lovers or roommates or friends that with *two* incomes there'll be no trouble swinging the purchase.

So it's easy to become a gentrifier. But the experience isn't all fun, and many who are glad they did it once say "Never again."

For one thing, eighteenth and nineteenth century houses were seldom built on anything resembling a proper foundation. But if the building is solid enough, so what? That blithe attitude lasts only until the happy new owners try to open the windows. Most of them probably won't budge. Those that do open, or can be pried open, may insist on staying that way. And the gorgeous marble-mantled fireplace may have to be only for looks, not use, because as the structure has settled, cracks have opened in the chimney flue. Obeying the laws of gravity, water will collect in sagging areas of the roof, but it won't stay there. Those peculiar oval patterns on the plaster ceilings are not some long-forgotten style of decor.

Many a gay gentrifier has lain awake through rainstorms, anxiously wondering if the contractor's costly roof patch job really *will* stop the leak in the grand salon, where the hand-painted rose garlands and plaster curlicues were just restored at such high cost to spinal cords and pocketbooks.

Our industrious duo will soon discover that practically nothing in a structure built fifty or more years ago conforms to today's standards. There's no point even looking at ready-made draperies or blinds; they'll all have to be made to order. The replacement hardware that will make it possible for the pocket door to slide in and out of the wall hasn't been manufactured in years. The niche intended for the refrigerator won't be big enough for current models. And on and on and on.

The smiling realtor *could* tell his pair of buyers that they will jolly well *need* two incomes – possibly more – to make their dream come true. And to keep it that way: the exposed brick walls may look charming, and so are all those big rooms with twelve-foot ceilings. But the heating bills will soon demonstrate that the insulating qualities of early nineteenth century brick are nil, and that there is indeed a rationale for smallish rooms with low ceilings.

And . . . anyone ever try to change a light bulb in a fixture that's hanging twelve or fourteen feet overhead?

But there are rewards. When the last of the paint has been applied – or removed, depending – what an impressive housewarming party it will be. The sore muscles, the dinners eaten on stacks of lumber and tasting of plaster dust, the hemorrhaging bank accounts – all this will be forgotten as the gentrifiers bask in their friends' admiring remarks and green glow of envy. Then all the effort will have been worth it. Until, that is, the next time it rains.

III. G.S.T.

G.S.T. stands for Gay Standard Time, which translates as late. Individually gay men vary in the matter of promptness about as much as any other humans, but when we get together, oh my dear.

A guest who's been invited for dinner at eight and actually shows up at that hour is likely to find his host answering the door sopping wet and with a towel around his waist. The ticket holder who arrives promptly at the big fundraiser will have to shiver in the cold until someone finally arrives to open the doors of the auditorium. Or else he will have to spend so much time at the bar that the show ends up as no more than a haze of noise and lights.

The heart of the matter may be simply that we are going to be with other gay people. And one of them may be Mr. Wonderful, or at least Mr. Next. Care must be taken, and whose hair is ever arranged just right? Besides, nobody else is going to be on time, either.

Perhaps we should try to clean up our act and mount a stirring nationwide campaign to promote Gay Promptness. After all, think of the hapless dinner guest, having to say to his wet and shivering host, "Er, I was on my way to have a drink right around the corner, and I thought I'd check to see if I could pick up some ice for you . . . or something," then having to leave and come back again later, feeling like a fool all the while.

Yes, wiping out G.S.T. would certainly benefit civilization in many ways. Still, we believe the custom should be left unmolested, and for four important reasons.

First, the loss of G.S.T. would radically cut into our primping time.

Second, lateness does have its charms: those who arrive at a gay function between the hour appointed for its beginning and its actual starting time can socialize, maybe have a drink or two, which is nice, and then, when things do get underway, everybody knows everybody and is in a lovely, mellow state of mind.

Third, it's impossible to make an entrance when one gets somewhere on time: the spectators haven't yet arrived.

Fourth, ending G.S.T. is a hopeless task. Defeat is certain. Who among us would have the time to organize the huge national campaign that would be necessary, with the fundraising Telethon and all? Nobody. And that's because tardiness takes time and effort, and we're all busy as hell being late somewhere for something.

IV. Opera Lovers

Not all gay men like opera; it only seems that way. We do enjoy the art form out of all proportion to our numbers. Some of us attend a few times a year, and others have a more serious interest in it; these are opera buffs. Those of us who like opera extravagantly are opera queens. Among this lot hides a tiny minority – the opera fiends.

The queens and fiends are hard to tell apart right off. They are both addicted to the art, perhaps since childhood, and maybe make gross financial sacrifices for season tickets or even a single performance. Neither can wait for the marvelous new recording of *Tal di Tale* with Whoozits singing the title role and O. Hurr conducting. Queens and fiends both know a good deal of opera history, long and complex as it is, and both will talk about opera until their friends begin to scream.

But there are certain differences. The opera fiend shows certain traits that are lacking in even the most emphatic opera queen. The main characteristic, the true mark of the fiend, is that, however gentlemanly he may be otherwise, on speaking about opera he will become entirely rude. He *cannot* discuss the subject in a calm manner. You can blandly agree with all he says, show how very impressed you are with his judgments, how enlightened by his knowledge, and he will still find some way to be nastily contradictory.

To observe this in its concentrated form, all that's necessary is to see two opera fiends talking to one another on their favorite subject. They snap and snarl so ferociously that it looks like assault and battery is only moments away. But listen carefully: beyond the opening skirmishes they are likely to enter into two almost separate monologues of contradiction and put-down. It only appears as though they're talking back and forth. The fact is, they can't. An opera fiend is never wrong. All judgments are absolute, final, and perfect.

This leads to another particular trait of the opera fiend: While he may be a mine of information on his favorite subject, the mine is likely to be salted. This is most noticeable when he presents as facts matters which are most likely to be undocumented: "Well, Mozart wrote that passage after he'd had a fight with his wife and a bad breakfast. And that was the week his cat died, too. Shows, don't you think?"

The opera fiend doesn't stop at playing fast and loose with the history of the art. To defend his position he will discuss minutely such matters as tempo and timbre, roulades and cadenzas, chest registers and head tones. But don't ask him to read a page of music, much less a whole score, or even pick out the simplest melody in C major on the piano.

A third trait that identifies the opera fiend is his relationship with the late Maria Callas. You can discover it merely by asking when he thinks she lost her voice. (Be sure you don't put this question to a Callas-queen, though; they're as loyal as Judy-queens: "Never! She was *always* wonderful. Now get out!") The true opera fiend, if he is old enough, will say it really began to go at some time *after* he heard her sing in person. If he's too young, then he will tell you that Maria's instrument started downhill *after* the date his favorite Callas recording was made.

And he'll bombard you with masses of his own personal information, dripping with technical terms, in discussing the effects of her nose job, her weight loss, her choice of repertoire, her wobble. Obviously his answer is the only possible one. But no two opera fiends will ever answer the same, not remotely.

The problem here is at the core of the functioning of the opera fiend. He has no real general basis for his feelings and preferences in opera, no consistency of taste. That's because, in truth, the opera fiend does not relate to opera in terms of esthetics, immediate enjoyment, or even historical interest. He has immersed himself in this art in a highly complex and emotional way because he finds it hard to relate to much else in life. For the opera fiend opera is an escape from loneliness, a punching-bag for personal problems, and a substitute for becoming involved with real people on a one-to-one basis.

Unlike the opera buff or opera queen, the opera fiend does not truly enjoy opera. He would like to, of course, but *when* is *any* conductor, stage director, or cast of singers *ever* going to be good enough?

Next time an opera fiend corners you in the lobby at intermission, resist the temptation to lead him on until he inevitably contradicts himself. Feign polite attention until you can graciously withdraw from his presence. After all, we who are not so afflicted should try to feel some compassion for the opera fiend; he's more to be pitied than scorned. After the performance ends, good, bad, or indifferent, you are going off to a pleasant evening, more than likely, and the opera fiend is returning home alone.

*

V. Daddy

That great rarity, a new role, has emerged in the urban gay scene in recent years. We speak of the Daddy, who is the first real addition to the gay pantheon of Sexy Types since the Biker, who dates from the fifties. The Daddy is not only new and rare but also a curious phenomenon: he's an authority figure surfacing in a time of gay liberation, and he functions successfully in a milieu that's extremely youth oriented and body conscious.

And by Daddy we don't mean Sugar Daddy. Nothing so squalid. We're talking about the older man who comes on as the sympathetic, sexy father-figure. Without trying too much to hide his age, he makes the effort to stay trim and together and look his best. As for "older," the Daddy will be forty and up, as a rule, though there are men in their middle to later thirties who play the role, almost always for a very young crowd.

Older-younger relationships have been around among gay people since forever, at least since they were institutionalized among the ancient Greeks. While the Hellenic ideal may not always be reached or even desired today, many older-younger couplings, brief or extended, are far less cynically exploitive than observers may believe.

As a specific role the Daddy appeared sometime in the seventies, and very likely derives from the gay sadomasochist subculture. There, experience and ability in playing a role are more valued than youth or looks. Dominant-submissive scenes, an essential expression of father-son relationships, are a commonplace of S&M sexual activity.

The first Daddy, as we imagine it, must have tired of whips-and-chains and decided one night to try something new. Dressed butch but not threateningly, he goes into a vanilla bar. It's full of pretty young men, but Daddy, accustomed to playing it indifferent, masculine, and serious, pays them little overt attention. Reactions vary: some of the guys, ever searching for the perfect pecs, hardly notice him, while others, perhaps to their own surprise, are intrigued. At least one of them decides he *must* get to know this butch stranger better. And Daddy doesn't go home alone.

The question is, if the role works well for older men, why

aren't more Daddies in evidence? It's doubtful that the saturation point has been reached.

Part of the answer lies in the fact that, like any role, it doesn't suit every person. A successful Daddy should not remind others of Mommie, but besides a definite maleness about him, he has to show a sympathetic interest in young men. He must be willing to listen a good deal and display concern for problems he himself hasn't fretted about in years.

However casual or intimate his relationships with younger men, the Daddy must keep up his role at all times. He isn't Daddy if he isn't strong and wise. He can't talk about *his* troubles, he can give advice but not ask for any, and he can't camp even a little, unless it's out in the woods with tents and bears and such.

While the role may be unsuitable for some and too demanding for others, probably the biggest reason for the low numbers of Daddies is that a man who assumes the role defines himself as . . . older. Very many gay men, of whatever age, do not care to cross that line. *Definitely* do not care to.

The Daddy gets little competition from other older man. Many of them, of course, prefer to associate with persons fairly close to their own age. And the others . . . Well, as a young man who likes older men says, "So many of them come on all wrong. They talk my ear off, never ask any questions, show no interest in anything about me except getting me into bed. I can get all that from young guys. It isn't what I'm looking for in older men."

Our young friend has hit on the Daddy's appeal. Simply, he plays father. We've pointed out earlier that the Distant Dad is all too common in the upbringings of gay men. As Joseph Campbell puts it in *The Hero with a Thousand Faces,*

> . . . if it had been a household in which the father had been of no force. . . [where there was] no one of masculine presence who could be honored and respected . . . the quest will have been for a decent father image . . . some sort of symbolic realization of . . . sonship to a father.

An older man who comes on with a younger man, but without playing Daddy, far from getting closer, essentially may be creating emotional distance between them, because he is reviving an unpleasant reality the young man may well have experienced with his real-life father. As our young friend says, "That isn't what I'm looking for. . . ."

Over the centuries gay men who felt the need have no doubt searched for father figures, and this may explain a good deal of the Daddy's appeal, but it doesn't help us to understand why this formalized expression in a definite role has appeared so recently in the gay world.

We can only guess that it may be a reaction to the weakening of the nuclear family, the prevalence of divorce, and the specifically American custom of getting the kids out of the house and on their own as soon as possible. Surely the sexual revolution has created a lot of gay men who are willing and eager to experiment with a wide range of sexual situations and roles, once they reach the "Everyone in the bars is so *alike*" stage. And the fast-lane gay scene, with its narrow range of pleasures and prizes, can fall short of answering a lot of needs and sometimes be a rather cold, tough place.

So here comes a man who knows how the world works, who's warm, comforting, and helpful. In addition he provides a guilt-free sexual *frisson*, of fulfilling the very common fantasy among gay men of getting it on with father.

Reasons for the appearance of this new Sexy Type may be complex, but it's pretty clear that there's a strong need for the Daddy. In a sense the role is older than history, but in this specific form, the Daddy is a role whose time has come.

VI. Dining Out Gay

Let's get something, er, straight: a restaurant that's gay owned and staffed is not necessarily a gay restaurant. The world is full of closeted eateries. A *gay* gay restaurant has certain unique characteristics.

A high level of innuendo is almost always present. The maitre d' is likely to greet a male couple with "How are *you guys* tonight?" implying that he's aware they're pausing for sustenance between bouts of endless flaming sex. A lone male on being seated will be told something like, "*Bobby* will *take care* of you this evening," as if Bobby were going to present his naked body instead of the menu.

Decor almost always goes to the extreme. The traditional

style brings together lots of mirrors, gilt, paneling, and, of course, chandeliers. Then there's the snowblind school, where everything is white white white, and of late the high-tech/stark chic approach that gives an odd banquet-in-a-factory effect to dining out.

Whatever the style, a fair number of gay restaurants have a less than perfect grip on their decor, obviously because funds for interior design ran out sooner than expected. One of our favorites is Buckingham Palace except for the chairs, which look like they came out of a bus station coffee shop.

Universally in *gay* gay restaurants, the tables are set with too much silver and too many glasses, a candle, and flowers. The effect is usually very pleasing to the eye, but unless the waiter removes the needless items, the table ends up an obstacle course for the diner.

Then there's the food. At the average gay restaurant the dining is more likely to be interesting than superb. This is especially the case where what's served is supposed to complement the decor, or, worse yet, live up to it. Food content may be rather arbitrarily selected, on the basis of color and texture and on construction potential.

Often enough this *Architectural Digest* approach to cooking is most visible when the diner orders the chef's special for the day, or the entree featured in a box of its own on the menu. It's sure to make the Taj Mahal look like a squashed milk carton in comparison. The customer should remember to avoid eating any little blinking lights found embedded in the food – they're strictly for decoration.

The lust for elegance is apparent in other ways as well. Hollandaise sauce, and lots of it, ends up on some extremely unlikely edibles, like roast duck, for instance. Veal scallops have been known to be drowned in orange sauce, and Cornish game hens are routinely stuffed with absolutely anything. Barbecued ribs come paired with veal Oscar, and that abomination, steak and lobster tail, is almost inevitable.

Some gay restaurants, trying to survive while serving only a minority of the general population, become quite schizophrenic. In attempting to appeal both to the formal diner and the late-night snack crowd ("We gotta get something to eat or we'll be bombed out of our minds"), the menu will look, well, bizarre. One side of it will feature alleged haute cuisine, and the other will list such items as burgers and fried onion rings.

Gay restaurants may not be perfect, but they're nice places to go with friends, and for travelers they offer a welcome alternative to sterile hotel eating places and plastic chains. And when mother visits, where else does she get such attentive service when you take her out for dinner?

Brunch. A special sort of gay dining experience is reserved for weekends, during the day. It's breakfast-plus-lunch, which equals brunch. The custom began among the idle rich, but it was taken up by gays early on, and has spread throughout the land. Everybody may be brunching nowadays, but we still have our very own approach to this tradition. And that makes brunch, however delightful, also very dangerous.

Here are some tips for a safe brunch.

First, the chef may be moonlighting and could be an amateur. He has to deal with a lot of orders in a short space of time. So usually it's best to stick to omelets and other standard items. If you want good eggs Benedict, give up in advance.

Next, there's drinking at brunch. Very often you are served champagne before and with your meal. So charming and Fred-and-Ginger. However, especially if you have a hangover, it is easy to find yourself holding a glass of bubbly in one hand and the Bloody Mary you ordered in the other, and sipping at them alternately. This of course is considered a bit gauche. As a friend said to his lover, "Why don't you just ask for a fifth of vodka and a straw?"

Then there's the service. Your waiter, remember, has also had a heavy night behind him, but he's gotten up early, has to deal with table after table of often out-of-sorts customers, and like the chef may be an aficionado, not a professional.

So your service can be hopeless and your server a real sourball. What to do? Well, you *can* make snide remarks, but it's doubtful that service will improve as a result. The thing to do is convince your waiter that it is worthwhile to wait on you and your party with élan and dispatch. Speaking as if you think he can't hear you, make a remark that holds out the possibility of some glittering prize coming his way. For New York or Los Angeles, the line could be something like, "That waiter of ours would be perfect in the massage scene with Redford at the end of the movie, except I'm not sure what his smile looks like." For other areas, adapt the remark to local conditions.

Don't always blame the waiter for slow service. Lift up your ears and listen: can strident voices be heard coming from the direction of the kitchen? If so, perhaps the omelet you're being so patient about is even now flying across the workspace.

Memorize these safe-brunch rules:

1. The fancier your food, the more toothpicks hidden in it.

2. Don't suddenly leap up and rush away from the table at the sight of food. This could start an ugly trend. Leave graciously, and don't sprint until you're out of sight of the other diners.

3. Don't brunch with anyone whose hangover, drugover, or guiltover is worse than yours, unless he's your lover, in which case a good deal of it is probably your fault.

The biggest danger of brunch comes at its end. That's when, comforted by food and soothed by champagne, you step out into the ghastly sunshine. You're about to part with your friends and return home, there to empty the cat box, pay bills, and do the laundry. Then a friend says, "Oh, let's have just one little drinky somewhere, okay?" Or maybe you say it.

A few cocktails later and it's high afternoon, and somebody in the crowd knows of a little bar show that's side-splitting, so. . . .

By sunset you're acidy-burpy, quite sauced, sitting in some bar that ordinarily you wouldn't be caught dead in, and asking yourself troubling questions: Where are my friends? Who is this man groping me so familiarly? Where is my car? Will my cat ever forgive me?

Brunch – a pleasure, but also a danger, mainly in that it's a waster of Sundays. But then, it's better to waste Sunday than have Sunday waste you.

YOU AND GAY TRADITIONS

16 Wild Horses

> ...we are carriers of lives and legends — who knows the unseen frescoes on the private walls of the skull?
>
> — William Goyen

In his *The Unrecorded Life of Oscar Wilde,* Rupert Croft-Cook writes that had Wilde not become involved in a lawsuit which led to his downfall, we might have a very different impression of him: "Oscar would have added success to success, probably ... He might have realised all his ambitions and become solidly rich, sent his sons to Eton, been knighted by the Queen ... in which case he would probably be remembered today as a minor playwright of the last century whose life, as a happily married man living in London, was of no particular interest."

This sums up the great problem in gay history: its records are comparatively few. It isn't hard to see why. Let's say that a gay man keeps a frank diary of his life and loves. When he dies, in 1785 or 1885 or 1985, what will happen to his diary? Most likely it will be destroyed by his heirs, usually his family, to avoid embarrassment and "protect his reputation." Lord Byron, poet and bisexual heart-throb of the early nineteenth century, bequeathed his memoirs to fellow poet Thomas Moore. This straight and rather straitlaced man was so shocked on reading the manuscript that he threw it into the fire.

Sometimes the whole is not destroyed, just the gay parts are. After the gay American poet Hart Crane died, his mother razored out "scandalous" and otherwise revealing passages from his letters before allowing them to be published.

Such information as we do have about gay people in the past is not exactly broadcast to all corners of the world. For instance, it's reasonably sure that these schoolbook heroes were gay: the explorer Ferdinand Magellan, composers George Frederick Handel and Franz Schubert, painters Velásquez and Delacroix, and those heroes of the American Revolution, Thomas Paine and Alexander Hamilton.

If you are surprised at any of these names being here, then you can see just how much history has been heterosexualized.

When evidence of gay life and culture can't be suppressed, it is minimized. Straight (or, sometimes, highly closeted) academics and historians have not cared to deal with their subjects as being gay. Beethoven as homosexual is discussed reluctantly because it has to be, due to his messy relationship with his nephew. (The fact that Ludwig was partly of African ancestry doesn't get much play, either.)

A century ago historians could excuse themselves by saying it was improper to discuss matters dealing with sexuality. More recently the reason for "leaving out the gay" has been that it doesn't matter what anyone does in bed anyway.

What facts about gay life are left, then? Over the years there has been a small amount of good and useful work, but much of what we know comes from police reports and court records. These give an essentially negative image of gay existence, and almost always from a straight point of view.

Generations of young gay people, finding little in bookstores and libraries that was informative, have turned to fiction. In novels by straights they found the campy or sinister stereotypes and little more, and for a long time specifically gay fiction was only marginally more enlightening. Most gay material lay between the lines, as in much of Proust, or was even further removed: is Somerset Maugham's *Of Human Bondage* really about a nice young medical student and his hangup on a trampy waitress? (The original of the Mildred character is supposed to have been a male hustler.)

Where gay life has been described directly, with a few exceptions it has been exploitive. A few chapters of realistic depiction may be present, but inevitably it all ends up as lurid scenes in low places. This genre came to its height (and, thankfully, a halt) with the so-called "Twilight World" paperback novels of the fifties and early sixties. They had such titles as *Shadows of Shame, Whisper His Sin, The World at Twilight*, and *Naked to the Night.* Whatever the plot, it was inevitable that a gay man died at the end, leaving his lover to mourn in celibacy or serve a jail sentence for murder. Even the few examples of the better class of gay novel, such as *Quatrefoil,* adhered to this moral formula. Sometimes, in slight variation, the gay man did not die; he went straight and married the Right Woman.

Today there is a wide choice of gay fiction and nonfiction, but this is a recent development. Until just yesterday, we have been a minority group without our own works of history. In this we differ from other groups, such as American blacks and Jews, both of whom have a body of historical work. This means they have not been in our position; that is, they have not had to try to puzzle out their story and their place in society from almost nothing but Ku Klux Klan pamphlets, reports of lynchings or pogroms, or the *Protocols of the Elders of Zion.*

In short, because gay history has been mostly in the hands of non-gay people, it has been suppressed, ignored, rationalized away, or just bluntly falsified. The claim that it doesn't matter what anybody does in bed has a suspiciously convenient ring of instant tolerance. If a historical figure's gay side is carefully disguised or minimized, isn't that obvious evidence that it *does* matter?

Certainly it matters. All this twiddling with history hardly adds to the self-esteem of gay people. Viewing homosexuality exclusively through straight eyes is hardly the way to avoid shame, self-hatred, the closet, self-destructive behavior, and suicide.

Setting things right

The truth is, in order to have history in a form undistorted by straight bias and questionable motives, we must be our own historians. Consider the gay history of your part of the world: what was gay life like a hundred years ago, even fifty years ago? A clear idea of it is probably very hard to develop.

We have made a good start. In the flood of gay books in the

last twenty years or so there have been some fine works, notably Jonathan Katz's *Gay American History*, whose bibliography shows what great efforts the author had to make to collect his information, and from what a wide array of sources.

If much of gay history is lost, more is being made every day. Few of us may be at the center of political or cultural activities, but each of us lives in his own space-time and has his own experiences, and sees life from his unique point of view. As James Baldwin wrote, "We are trapped in history, and history is trapped in us."

Still, many of us might feel we have little to offer. The closest thing many of us have to letters is a stack of phone bills, and the custom of diary-keeping has almost died out. But lots of other things will tell future generations about us: scrapbooks of photographs showing friends and gay events, collections of lapel buttons, gay periodicals. These are the kinds of items that just "pile up." All too often they get thrown out.

A friend of ours, in the process of moving, discovered several hundred flyers and programs he had put aside long before. Most of them concerned charity and drag affairs held in his city, some as far back as the thirties. He timidly offered them to a gay archive, and its representatives fell all over themselves to accept the collection. As they explained to him, many of the items were the only copies known, and some could be used to trace the beginnings of local gay political activity.

Our friend was asked to do some interviews on tape for an oral history project. He was surprised at this as well, but as he came to realize, the memories of older gay men are sometimes the only sources for a good deal of gay life as lived earlier in this century.

Even where there is no local gay archives or history project, anybody can tape his memories at home on cassettes, at very small expense. Many people who would never write out anything find that talking of the past is very easy.

Younger gay men can contribute too. With the rise of gay liberation and an increase in social and political activities, a great deal of material has been generated.

The idea of gay archives is not new. Much documentation was collected early in this century by Magnus Hirschfeld at his Institute for Sexual Science, in Berlin. Unfortunately for our history, the Institute was sacked and destroyed by Nazi troops in 1935, and Hirschfeld died in exile not long after.

The gay archives that exist today are nonprofit institutions, and of course are underfunded. If you have a lot of extremely rare items, some purchase arrangement may be possible, but ordinarily it's unrealistic to expect to make a wad selling material to an archive. Contributions may be tax-deductible, however.

The man who wishes upon his death to leave money or materials to gay archives should be sure to have a will specifically providing for this. If you intend that papers, diaries, scrapbooks and the like be contributed, it may not always be wise to depend on the executor. The great bulk of gay history, remember, has been destroyed by relatives worried about "reputation" and "family name." An alternative is to leave all one's personal papers, diaries, journals, or whatever to a trusted gay friend, with the expressed wish that items useful to the archives later be turned over to them.

If the donor himself feels that some of his material, such as an extremely frank diary, could cause hurt or embarrassment, it's possible to arrange limitations on use, or to specify that it remain sealed for a given number of years.

At this writing there are fifteen or more gay archives in this country. Most large cities have one, sometimes several, though the South at this point is undersupplied.

Archives are listed in local gay publications and in the *Gayellow Pages* directories.

By preserving our history we pass on to future generations not only a record of gay life past, but also a sense of pride and worth, not of shame. For this alone, gay history has an enormous importance.

☐ **IN SUCH DARK PLACES,** by Joseph Caldwell, $7.00. This impressive novel about a not-so-liberated gay man's conflict with love and faith, isolation and commitment, was praised by *Saturday Review* for its "vivid portraits and unforgettable scenes." By Joseph Caldwell, winner of the Rome Prize.

☐ **THE ALEXANDROS EXPEDITION,** by Patricia Sitkin, $6.00. When Evan Talbot leaves on a mission to rescue an old schoolmate who has been imprisoned by fanatics in the Middle East, he doesn't realize that the trip will also involve his own coming out and the discovery of who it is that he really loves.

☐ **ALL-AMERICAN BOYS,** by Frank Mosca, $5.00. "I've known that I was gay since I was thirteen. Does that surprise you? It didn't me. . . ." So begins *All-American Boys,* the story of a teenage love affair that should have been simple — but wasn't.

☐ **THE MOVIE LOVER,** by Richard Friedel, $7.00. The entertaining coming-out story of Burton Raider, who is so elegant that as a child he reads *Vogue* in his playpen. "The writing is fresh and crisp, the humor often hilarious," writes the *L.A. Times.*

☐ **CHINA HOUSE,** by Vincent Lardo, $5.00. This gay gothic romance/mystery has everything: two handsome lovers, a mysterious house on the hill, sounds in the night, and a father-son relationship that's closer than most.

☐ **DANNY,** by Margaret Sturgis, $7.00. High school teacher Tom York has a problem when the school board wants to censor many of the books he feels are most important for his classes to read. But all that pales in the face of the new difficulties that arise when he finds himself in an intense love affair with Danny, his most promising student.

☐ **FRANNY: The Queen of Provincetown,** by John Preston, $5.00. Even if you dressed Franny in full leather, he would still look like a queen. It's the way he walks, his little mannerisms, and his utter unwillingness to change them or hide them that give him away. "The best gay male novel of the year," writes *The Front Page,* Raleigh, N.C.

☐ **I ONCE HAD A MASTER and other tales of erotic love,** by John Preston, $8.00. One of this country's best-known writers of erotic gay male fiction here tells the story of a man's journey through the S/M world, beginning with another man as his master and ending in that role himself.

☐ **IN THE TENT,** by David Rees, $6.00. Seventeen-year-old Tim realizes that he is attracted to his classmate Aaron, but, still caught up in the guilt of a Catholic upbringing, he has no idea what to do about it until a camping trip results in unexpected closeness.

☐ **THE HUSTLER,** by John Henry Mackay; trans. by Hubert Kennedy, $8.00. Gunther is fifteen when he arrives alone in the Berlin of the 1920s. There he is soon spotted by Hermann Graff, a sensitive and naive young man who becomes hopelessly enamored with Gunther. But love does not fit neatly into Gunther's new life.... *The Hustler* was first published in 1926. For today's reader, it combines a poignant love story with a colorful portrayal of the gay subculture that thrived in Berlin a half-century ago.

☐ **SOCRATES, PLATO AND GUYS LIKE ME: Confessions of a gay schoolteacher,** by Eric Rofes, $7.00. When Eric Rofes began teaching sixth grade at a conservative private school, he soon felt the strain of a split identity. Here he describes his two years of teaching from within the closet, and his difficult decision to finally come out.

☐ **MURDER IS MURDER IS MURDER,** by Samuel M. Steward, $7.00. Gertrude Stein and Alice B. Toklas go sleuthing through the French countryside, attempting to solve the mysterious disappearance of their neighbor, the father of their handsome gardener. A new and very different treat from the author of the Phil Andros stories.

☐ **ONE TEENAGER IN TEN: Writings by gay and lesbian youth,** edited by Ann Heron, $4.00. One teenager in ten is gay; here, twenty-six young people tell their stories: of coming to terms with being different, of the decision how – and whether – to tell friends and parents, and what the consequences were.

☐ **DANCER DAWKINS AND THE CALIFORNIA KID,** by Willyce Kim, $6.00. Dancer Dawkins views life best from behind a pile of hotcakes. Her lover, Jessica Riggins, has fallen into the clutches of Fatin Satin Aspen. Meanwhile, Little Willie Gutherie of Bangor, Maine, renames herself The California Kid, stocks up on Rubbles Dubble bubble gum, and heads west. When this crew collides in San Francisco, what can be expected? Just about anything....

☐ **CHOICES,** by Nancy Toder, $7.00. This popular novel about lesbian love depicts the joy, passion, conflicts and intensity of love between women as Nancy Toder conveys the fear and confusion of a woman coming to terms with her sexual and emotional attraction to other women.

☐ **THE PEARL BASTARD,** by Lillian Halegua, $4.00. Frankie is fifteen when she leaves her large, suffocating Catholic family. Here, with painful innocence and acute vision, she tells the story of her sudden entry into a harsh maturity, beginning with the man in the fine green car who does not mourn the violent death of a seagull against his windshield.

☐ **SECOND CHANCES,** by Florine de Veer, $7.00. Is it always harder to accept what is offered freely? Jeremy could easily have the love of his devoted friend Roy, yet he chooses to pursue the handsome and unpredictable Mark instead.

☐ **THE BUTTERSCOTCH PRINCE,** by Richard Hall, $5.00. When Cordell's best friend and ex-lover is murdered, the only clue is one that the police seem to consider too kinky to follow up on. So Cordell decides to track down the killer himself – with results far different from what he had expected.

☐ **A DIFFERENT LOVE,** by Clay Larkin, $5.00. There have been heterosexual romance novels for years; now here's a gay one. When Billy and Hal meet in a small midwestern town, they feel sure that their love for each other is meant to last. But then they move to San Francisco, and the temptations of city life create complications they haven't had to face before.

☐ **KINDRED SPIRITS,** edited by Jeffrey M. Elliot, $7.00. Science fiction offers an almost unlimited opportunity for writers to explore alternative ways of living; in these twelve stories, the reader has a chance to see twelve very different visions of what it could mean to be gay or lesbian in other worlds and other times.

☐ **THE TWO OF US,** by Larry Uhrig, $7.00. The author draws on his years of counseling with gay people to give some down-to-earth advice about what makes a relationship work. He gives special emphasis to the religious aspects of gay unions.

☐ **LIFETIME GUARANTEE,** by Alice Bloch, $7.00. Here is the personal and powerfully-written chronicle of a woman faced with the impending death of her sister from cancer, at the same time that she must also face her family's reaction to her as a lesbian.

☐ **THE LAVENDER COUCH,** by Marny Hall, $8.00. Here is a guide to the questions that should be considered by lesbians or gay men considering therapy or who are already in it: How do you choose a good therapist? What kind of therapy is right for you? When is it time to leave therapy?

☐ **REFLECTIONS OF A ROCK LOBSTER: A story about growing up gay,** by Aaron Fricke, $5.00. When Aaron Fricke took a male date to the senior prom, no one was surprised: he'd gone to court to be able to do so, and the case had made national news. Here Aaron tells his story, and shows what gay pride can mean in a small New England town.

☐ **DECENT PASSIONS,** by Michael Denneny, $7.00. What does it mean to be in love? Do the joys outweigh the pains? Those are some of the questions explored here as Denneny talks separately with each member of three unconventional relationships – a gay male couple, a lesbian couple, and an interracial couple – about all the little things that make up a relationship.

☐ **YOUNG, GAY AND PROUD,** edited by Sasha Alyson, $4.00. Here is the first book ever to address the needs and problems of a mostly invisible minority: gay youth. Questions about coming out to parents and friends, about gay sexuality and health care, about finding support groups, are all answered here; and several young people tell their own stories.

☐ **HOT LIVING: Erotic stories about safer sex,** edited by John Preston, $8.00. The AIDS crisis has encouraged gay men to look for new and safer forms of sexual activity; here, over a dozen of today's most popular gay writers erotically portray those new possibilities.

☐ **CLASSIFIED AFFAIRS,** by John Preston and Frederick Brandt, $7.00. How do you write a personal ad that really will catch people's attention? What should you expect when you place an ad? When you reply? Here are answers to all those questions, and more – interspersed with numerous actual ads that the authors found memorable, funny or intriguing.

☐ **GAY AND GRAY,** by Raymond M. Berger, $8.00. Working from questionnaires and case histories, Berger has provided the closest look ever at what it is like to be an older gay man. For some, he finds, age has brought burdens; for others, it has brought increased freedom and happiness.

☐ **THE SPARTAN,** by Don Harrison, $6.00. In the days of the first Olympics, gay relationships were a common and valued part of life. *The Spartan* tells the story of a young athlete and his adventures in love and war, providing a vivid picture of classical Greece, the early Olympics, and an important part of our history.

☐ **$TUD,** by Phil Andros; introduction by John Preston, $7.00. Phil Andros is a hot and horny hustler with a conscience, pursuing every form of sex – including affection – without apology, yet with a sense of humor and a golden rule philosophy. When Sam Steward wrote these stories back in the sixties, they elevated gay fiction to new heights; today they remain as erotic and delightful as ever.

☐ **QUATREFOIL,** by James Barr, introduction by Samuel M. Steward, $7.00. Originally published in 1950, this book marks a milestone in gay writing: it introduced two of the first non-stereotyped gay characters to appear in American fiction. This story of two naval officers who become lovers gave readers of the fifties a rare chance to counteract the negative imagery that surrounded them.

Get this book FREE!

Personal classifieds are an increasingly popular way to meet people these days. In their book *Classified Affairs,* John Preston and Frederick Brandt take a look at the gay male personals. Here's everything you need to know about how to write a personal that really attracts attention, and what to expect when you place, or answer, an ad. Interspersed with the text are dozens of the most memorable classifieds you'll ever read.

Normally $7.00, *Classified Affairs* is yours **free** when you order any three other books described here. Just check the box at the bottom of the order form on the next page.

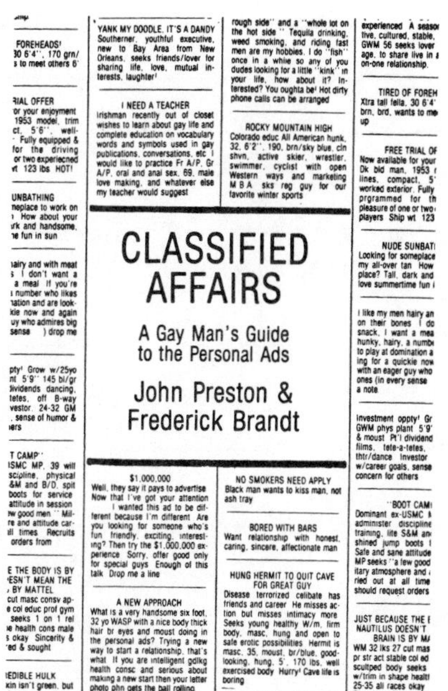